P

HONG KONG

TOP SIGHTS · LOCAL EXPERIENCES

LORNA PARKES, PIERA CHEN,
THOMAS O'MALLEY

Contents

Plan Your Trip 4

Tian Tan Buddha (p68)
HATCHAPONG PALURTCHAIVONG / SHUTTERSTOCK ©

Welcome to Hong Kong

Legendary for its harbour and iconic skyline, Hong Kong perpetually pushes the boundaries with its architecture, food and shopping scenes. Yet peel back the layers of mega-modernity and there are beguiling pockets to discover – temples wreathed in incense, neighbourhoods clinging to traditions and packed dim sum parlours – framed by lush, protected peaks and surf-beaten beaches.

Man Mo Temple (p72)
SANGHAI LOUNGROONG / GETTY IMAGES ©

Top Sights

Star Ferry

A world-class water ride. **p36**

FEDOR SELIVANOV / SHUTTERSTOCK ©

Victoria Peak

Breathtaking views from a natural skyscraper. **p38**

Man Mo Temple

Hong Kong Island's biggest temple. **p72**

Tian Tan Buddha

Enormous Buddha in Lantau's hills. **p68**

Temple Street Night Market
Food, fun and fortune-tellers. **p144**

Tai Kwun
Hollywood Rd's new heritage **p54**

Tsim Sha Tsui East Promenade
The best stroll in Hong Kong. **p124**

Chi Lin Nunnery
Serene complex of Kowloon temples. **p140**

LEFT: ASIANDREAM / GETTY IMAGES © RIGHT: PAULWONG / SHUTTERSTOCK ©

LEFT: LEE YIU TUNG / SHUTTERSTOCK © RIGHT: MHUNNEE / SHUTTERSTOCK ©

Ping Shan Heritage Trail

A well-preserved ancient walled village. **p156**

Hong Kong Park

Hillside oasis of engaging attractions. **p88**

LEFT: GIONNIXXX / GETTY IMAGES ©; RIGHT: MANFRED GOTTSCHALK / GETTY IMAGES ©

LEFT: H-AB / SHUTTERSTOCK ©; RIGHT: SEAONWEB / SHUTTERSTOCK ©

Ruins of the Church of St Paul, Macau

Macau's most iconic sight. **p162**

Sai Kung Peninsula

Home to a Unesco-listed geopark. **p158**

Eating

One of the world's most delicious cities, Hong Kong offers culinary excitement whether you're spending HK$50 on a bowl of noodles or HK$2000 on a seafood feast. And its food scene is the most diverse in all of Asia.

Dining Local

Cantonese cuisine

The dominant cuisine in Hong Kong. Many of China's top chefs fled to the territory around 1949; it was therefore here and not in its original home, Guǎngzhōu, that Cantonese cuisine flourished. It is characterised by an insistence on freshness, and flavours that are delicate and balanced.

Dai pai dong (大牌檔; pictured above) After WWII the colonial government issued food-stall licences to the families of injured or deceased civil servants. They came to be known as *dai pai dong* (meaning 'big licence stalls'). Traditionally, they are open-air hawker-style places, but many have been relocated. Dishes run the gamut from congee to seafood and sandwiches.

Cha chaan tang (茶餐廳; teahouses) Cheap and cheery neighbourhood eateries that appeared in the 1940s serving western-style snacks and drinks. Their menus have since grown to include more substantial Chinese and 'soy sauce western' dishes. They're famed for their pineapple buns and French toast.

Best Budget Eats

Kau Kee Pull up a plastic pew at this holy grail for beef brisket noodle soup fans. (p47)

Yat Lok Michelin-starred greasy roast goose heaven approved by Anthony Bourdain. (p46)

Chi Lin Vegetarian Refined Chinese veggie dishes in an ornamental garden. (p141)

Tai Cheong Bakery Serving Hong Kong's favourite egg tarts for half a century. (p46)

Best Midrange

Little Bao Hong Kong's most raved about fusion invention is this fist-sized Asian burger bao. (p61)

Old Bailey Exquisite Shanghainese dishes in an

KENNETH IP / SHUTTERSTOCK ©

architect-designed space. (p60)

Black Salt Creative takes on South Asian food, presented as scrumptious sharing dishes. (p81)

Spring Deer This old-timer of Northern Chinese cooking always delivers. (p135)

Aberdeen Fish Market Yee Hope Seafood Restaurant Seafood feast inside a wholesale fish market. (p119)

Best Fine Dining

Seventh Son Top-notch dim sum and Cantonese fare. (p100)

Rōnin Inventive Japanese dishes; counter seating only. (p47)

Duddell's Refined Cantonese cuisine in a cool, gallery-worthy space. (p49)

Bo Innovation Michelin-starred molecular Chinese cuisine for foodies. (p101)

Best Food Tours

Little Adventures in Hong Kong Guided walks led by food writers and chefs. (www.littleadventuresin hongkong.com)

Hong Kong Foodie Tour Regular group crawls to local food joints with native guides. (www.hongkong foodietours.com)

Humid with a Chance of Fishballs Guided dim sum lunches and craft breweries tours. (www.humidwith achanceoffishballs.com)

Top Tips

○ Most restaurants (midrange or above) take reservations. At popular addresses booking is crucial, especially for weekend dinners.

○ Many restaurants in Central have lunch specials.

○ Tipping is not a must as every bill (except at the cheapest Cantonese joints) includes a 10% service charge.

Hong Kong on a Plate
Dim Sum

Char siu bao is Hong Kong's classic barbecue pork bun.

Other staples include molten custard buns and chicken feet in black bean sauce.

Each dish, often containing two to four morsels steamed in a bamboo basket, is meant to be shared.

Har gow, translucent steamed parcels of chunky chopped shrimp.

Siu mai has a thicker skin encasing minced pork, topped with fish roe.

C_YUNG / GETTY IMAGES ©

★ Top Places for Dim Sum

Dim Sum in Hong Kong

Dim sum are Cantonese tidbits consumed with tea for breakfast or lunch. The term literally means 'to touch the heart' and the act of eating dim sum is referred to as yum cha, meaning 'to drink tea'.

In old-style dim sum places, just stop the waiter and choose something from the cart. Modern venues often give you an order slip. However, as dim sum dishes are often ready-made, the waiters should be able to show you samples to choose from.

Dim sum selection

DISION / GETTY IMAGES ©

Drinking & Nightlife

Energetic Hong Kong knows how to party. You can find any type of bar or pub you want (often hidden inside skyscrapers), but boozing will cost you dearly as alcohol is one of the only things that's taxed in this city: follow the happy hours, usually between 3pm and 8pm depending on the venue.

Dress Code

Smart casual is usually good enough for most evenings out, but patrons wearing shorts and flip-flops will not be admitted. Hong Kong's clubbers can be style-conscious, so dress to impress! The dressiest area is Central.

Drink Trends

Whisky, sake, gin and craft beer are all having their moment in Hong Kong and a growing number of bars are dedicated to connoisseurship of one particular drink. Expect hand-carved ice, obscure bottles and nerdily expert bartenders – and some of the best cocktail bars in the world.

Best Cocktail Bars

Quinary Justifiably lauded as one of the world's top bars, with Instagram-ready Asian-accented cocktails. (p62)

Old Man Intimate, hidden and serving ground-breaking cocktail concoctions. (p63)

Iron Fairies Magical drinking den channelling an old industrial vibe. (pictured above; p57)

Executive Bar Exclusive whisky and cocktail bar with serious Japanese mixology action. (p104)

Best Alcohol-Free

Peninsula Hong Kong The most elegant afternoon tea in the territory. (p136)

Teakha Wake up and smell the jasmine at this graceful tea lounge. (p83)

Lock Cha Tea Shop Antiquey environs and traditional music accompany tea here in Hong Kong Park. (p97)

Lan Fong Yuen The classic spot to try Hong Kong's famous milk tea. (p46)

Cupping Room Single-origin brews and a roastery in Tai Ping Shan. (p83)

Best Views

Sevva Beautiful people and beautiful harbour views by the HSBC Building. (p50)

SOUTH CHINA MORNING POST / CONTRIBUTOR / GETTY IMAGES ©

Skye Bar Magnificent harbour views, hidden on the roof of a Causeway Bay hotel. (p102)

Ben's Back Beach Bar Overlooking a deserted Shek O beach. (p120)

Cé La Vi Get right amid the business towers at this rooftop party bar in LKF. (p57)

Sugar Dizzying views from atop an Island East hotel. (p104)

Intercontinental Lobby Lounge Floor-to-ceiling glass overlooks Victoria Harbour. (p137)

Best Vibes

Pontiac American-style dive bar with class and good tunes. (p64)

Ping Pong Gintoneria Gin swigging in a former ping-pong hall. (p83)

Second Draft Local beers are the star at this comfy neighbourhood gastropub. (p102)

Bound Boho Kowloon hang-out with craft beer and art. (p153)

Worth a Trip

This town needs...more underground music venues like this. **This Town Needs** (www.facebook.com/thistownneeds; 1st fl, 6 Shung Shun St, Yau Tong; local bands HK$150, overseas HK$200-500; Yau Tong, exit A2) stages 10 to 15 gigs monthly in a hip warehouse space in the coastal Kowloon 'burb of Yau Tong. Formerly known as Hidden Agenda, it has expanded and rebranded to offer an exhibition space, movie screenings and cafe (noon to 7pm, days vary) as well as a bar during live shows. For up-to-date listings, go to its Facebook page. The entrance is one door to the west of the flashy Ocean One apartment building entrance.

Shopping

Hong Kong is renowned as a place of neon-lit retail pilgrimage. All international brands worth their logos have stores here, but there's also an increasing number of creative local designers and retail trailblazers. Together they are Hong Kong's shrines and temples to style and consumption.

Clothing

The best places to find global designer brands and luxury stores are the high-end malls around Central, Admiralty and Causeway Bay. Some shops, such as Prada, have discount outlets at Horizon Plaza (p120). Central and Wan Chai have some fabulous local designer boutiques; the streets around Tai Ping Shan St in Sheung Wan do too, and are a little more affordable.

Antiques

Hong Kong is one of the best markets in the world to shop for genuine Chinese antiques. That said, forgeries and expert reproductions abound, and serious buyers should restrict themselves to reputable antique shops and auction houses, and ask for certification that proves authenticity. Shops are concentrated around Hollywood Rd and the area between Tai Ping Shan St and Upper Lascar Row (Cat St).

Tech Hunting

There are fewer and fewer bargains to be had on the latest electronics gear in Hong Kong (and if you think you've found one, beware). Prices are certainly extremely competitive, though, and Hong Kong has a plethora of specialist shops and big chains. For reputable electronics centres, head to Wan Chai or Kowloon; Sham Shui Po is the place to go for cut-price computer centres.

DANIEL FUNG / SHUTTERSTOCK ©

Best Fashion

Kapok Hipster fashions from local and international designers. (p106)

Horizon Plaza Cut-rates on luxury goods and clothing in a 27-floor warehouse. (p120)

Pacific Place Ultra-luxe international clothing and accessories. (pictured above; p106)

Best Gifts

PMQ A one-stop-shop for affordable local design, fashion and jewellery. (p66)

Temple Street Night Market Everything from chopsticks to jewellery – bargain hard. (p144)

G.O.D. Playful accessories and homewares paying homage to Hong Kong pop culture. (p66)

Yue Hwa Chinese Products Emporium Old Chinese department store with embroidered slippers, chopsticks and calligraphy equipment. (p154)

Lam Kie Yuen Tea Co Venerable tea shop with huge selection. (p75)

Best Electronics

Wan Chai Computer Centre A warren of all things electronic. (p107)

Golden Computer Arcade Computers and components for extra-low prices. (p155)

Apliu Street Flea Market A huge digital-products flea market. (p155)

Top Tips

o There's no sales tax in Hong Kong, so ignore the 'Tax Free' signs in some stores.

o Many shops will package and post large items for you.

o Some imported goods have a Hong Kong–only guarantee, or one that's only valid in the country of manufacture.

Activities

Despite the metropolis of glass and steel at its heart, Hong Kong is an outdoorsy city offering countless ways to enjoy the water and the outlandish natural environment that pushes against the city's urban spaces. Hiking trails abound, there's a thriving keep-fit culture and dozens of spas and massage centres cater for relaxation-seekers.

Hiking

Many visitors are surprised to learn that Hong Kong is an excellent place for hiking. Lengthy wilderness trails criss-cross the territory and its islands through striking mountain, coast and jungle terrain. The four main ones are the **MacLehose Trail**, at 100km the longest in the territory; the 78km-long **Wilson Trail**, which runs on both sides of Victoria Harbour; the 70km-long **Lantau Trail**; and the **Hong Kong Trail** (p39), which is 50km long. Hong Kong's excellent public-transport network makes it feasible to tackle these trails a section at a time.

Water Sports

Hong Kong is defined by water and there are no shortage of water-based activities on the fringes of the city, particularly around the Sai Kung Peninsula in the New Territories where a number of scuba diving, wakeboarding and kayaking operators are based. The best time for windsurfing is October to December.

Best Hikes

Tai Long Wan Hiking Trail A glorious hike to an even more glorious beach. (p159)

Tai Tam Waterworks Heritage Trail Nature and history come together. (p118)

Dragon's Back Hong Kong Island's best scenery, running through Shek O. (pictured above; p117)

Morning Trail A shady paved path around the Peak, with stunning city views. (p39)

Best Beaches

South Bay A gem of a beach embraced by Hong Kong's French expatriate community. (p111)

FS11 / SHUTTERSTOCK ©

Middle Bay Popular with scenesters, this quaint little beach lies between Repulse Bay and South Bay. (p111)

St Stephen's Beach A delightful bolt-hole close to Stanley main beach, but without the crowds. (p111)

Shek O Beach Shady, sandy and framed by rocks. (p115)

Best Watery Escapades

Hong Kong Dolphin-watch Seek out Hong Kong's bubble-gum-pink dolphins in the Pearl River estuary. (p133)

Aqua Luna Set sail on a timbered junk boat to experience Victoria Harbour with local fanfare. (p46)

Sai Kung Scuba diving, kayaking and blue water galore. (p158)

Resources

○ Environmental Protection Department (www.epd.gov.hk) Lists country and marine parks.

○ Hong Kong Tourism Board (www.discover hongkong.com) Full list of sporting events.

○ Leisure and Cultural Services Department (www.lcsd.gov.hk) Lists of fields, stadiums, beaches, swimming pools, water-sports centres etc, including equipment for hire.

○ Enjoy Hiking (www.hiking.gov.hk) Government site with comprehensive information; select trails by area, level of difficulty, duration etc.

Architecture

Over the centuries Hong Kong has played host to everything from Taoist temples and Qing dynasty forts to Victorian churches and Edwardian hotels. The rapidity of construction has meant much of the charmingly old has been eagerly replaced by modern marvels, but preservation is starting to move up the agenda.

Traditional Chinese

About the only examples of precolonial Chinese architecture left in urban Hong Kong are Tin Hau temples and the Hung Shing temples that date from the early to mid-19th century, including those at Yau Ma Tei, Wan Chai and Ap Lei Chau. For anything more substantial, go to the New Territories to see walled villages, fortresses and ancient pagodas.

Colonial Architecture

Most of what is left of colonial architecture is on Hong Kong Island, especially in Central, though Tsim Sha Tsui on the Kowloon Peninsula is also home to quite a few examples. Much of Hong Kong and Macau's colonial architecture features adaptations for the tropical climate, such as typhoon-resistant roof tiles, just as some Chinese buildings have western-style motifs.

Modern Architecture

Enthusiasts of modern architecture will have a field day in Hong Kong. Central and Wan Chai are wonderful showcases for modern and contemporary buildings – many designed by internationally celebrated architects. Some of Macau's megacasinos must be seen to be believed.

EWILDING / SHUTTERSTOCK ©

Best Modern Architecture

HSBC Building The Norman Foster masterpiece commands a special place in the city's hearts and minds. (p44)

Bank of China Tower Some scoff at IM Pei's ingenious design as a futuristic meat cleaver. (p41)

Asia Society Hong Kong Centre A beautiful roof garden grows out of an overgrown former military site. (p94)

Lippo Centre 'Hugging Koalas' was designed by American architect, Paul Rudolph. (p96)

Best Colonial Architecture

Tai Kwun Complex of stern neoclassical edifices with Chinese roofs. (p54)

Old Supreme Court The most imposing colonial edifice left in town, though perhaps not the most beautiful. (p41)

PMQ Soho's old married police quarters is now a multistorey modernist retail and arts haven. (p66)

Former Marine Police Headquarters Blatant commercialism cannot detract from the poise and beauty of this neoclassical monument. (pictured above; p132)

St John's Cathedral Criticised for blighting the colony's landscape when it was first built. (p41)

Béthanie Two octagonal cow sheds plus a neo-Gothic chapel equal a performing-arts space. (p114)

Best Chinese Architecture

Pak Sing Ancestral Hall An 1856 Sheung Wan temple built to store corpses awaiting burial in China. (p78)

Tin Hau Temple A fine Tin Hau Temple that has kept much of its original elements. (p94)

Chi Lin Nunnery A meticulous modern replica of Tang dynasty Buddhist architecture. (p140)

Man Mo Temple Creaking, heady-scented behemoth on Hollywood Rd. (p72)

Traditional Culture

Thanks to its different trajectory of development from the rest of China, Hong Kong has a hybrid culture that is as complex as it is fascinating. Colonisation has westernised the city, yet the influences of traditional Lingnan culture, dominant in Guǎngdōng and other areas of Southern China, are still very much apparent.

ESCHCOLLECTION / GETTY IMAGES ©

Best for Indigenous

Aberdeen & Ap Lei Chau The Water People's culture is palpable at markets, food stalls, and on dragon boats. (p119)

Pok Fu Lam Village An old way of life among relics of a dairy and a fire dragon. (p117)

Yau Ma Tei Kowloon's grassroots street culture is still very much alive at places like Tin Hau Temple. (p147)

Best for Local

Hong Kong Museum of History All about Hong Kong: birth, teething, growing pains and all. (p130)

North Point Hong Kong's Little Fújiàn, particularly evocative at Chun Yeung Street Market. (p94)

Cantonese opera The endangered Unesco-listed art is conserved at the Sunbeam, Yau Ma Tei and Ko Shan theatres. (p147)

Mahjong Parlours Where hardcore players gather for a game of mahjong. (pictured above; p155)

Best for Food

Mido Café Atmospheric 1950s *cha chaan tang*, with retro tiles and all the works. (p152)

Luk Yu Tea House Vintage Eastern art deco interiors and Lingnan-style paintings. (p49)

Australia Dairy Company Solid *cha chaan tang* staples served with surly efficiency. (p152)

Kung Lee Feeding the neighbourhood sugarcane juice since 1948. (p65)

Tai O

If you're going to Lantau to see the Big Buddha, add on a trip to Tai O on the island's far-flung west coast. On weekends, droves of visitors trek here to see the historical home of the Tanka boat people with houses built on stilts above the ocean. Take bus 1 from Mui Wo, 11 from Tung Chung, or 21 from Ngong Ping on Lantau to get here.

KINGROBERT / SHUTTERSTOCK ©

Parks & Gardens

Between Hong Kong's urban mono-liths, the city is dressed with some very decent parks and gardens – bolt-holes for frazzled city workers, open spaces for families and reminders that Hong Kong is a subtropical territory where nature is never far away.

Best for a Picnic

Victoria Peak Garden The peak above the Peak. This landscaped haven of calm commands untrammelled views. (p39)

Hong Kong Park A rainforest-like aviary and the city's oldest colonial building lie in this leisure space. (p88)

Waterfall Bay Park Deities, a lovely cascade and fishing junks in the sea at Pok Fu Lam. (pictured above; p116)

Best Urban Oases

Hong Kong Zoological & Botanical Gardens Enveloped by skyscrapers, this stronghold of nature has graced the city since 1871. (p45)

Cheung Kong Park A petite oasis favoured by lunching office workers in the middle of Central. (p41)

Kowloon Park A welcome swath of green with swimming facilities off busy Nathan Rd. (p130)

Best for Entertainment

Nan Lian Garden A splendid Tang-style garden at Chi Lin Nunnery, adorned with a pagoda, tea pavilion, koi pond and Buddhist pines. (p141)

Kowloon Walled City Park Former sin city reincarnated as a traditional Jiāngnán garden. (p150)

Ocean Park A huge aquarium and thrilling rides draw families to this highly popular amusement park. (p115)

Top Tips

○ All public parks have toilets and some have simple food stalls. Smoking is not allowed in parks, and most don't allow dogs either.

○ The Leisure & Cultural Services Department website (www.lcsd.gov.hk) lists the city's public parks and gardens.

For Kids

In a city where skyscrapers tower over city streets, subtropical trees swoop low, and excellent museums are connected by characterful trams and ferries, there's a lot for kids to get excited about. Food and sanitation are of a high standard, but crowds, traffic and pollution might spook more timid mini travellers.

SEAN PAVONE / SHUTTERSTOCK ©

Best Museums

Hong Kong Science Museum Three storeys of action-packed displays and a theatre. (p130)

Hong Kong Museum of History Brings the city's history to life in visually and aurally colourful ways. (p130)

Hong Kong Space Museum & Theatre Buttons to push, telescopes to peer through, simulation rides and computer quizzes. (p132)

Hong Kong Maritime Museum Exquisite ship models, real treasures salvaged from shipwrecks, and marine conservation. (p44).

Best Parks

Ocean Park Hong Kong's premier amusement park

has a top-notch aquarium and a cable-car ride overlooking the sea. (p115)

Hong Kong Park Turtles inhabit the ponds and the forest-like aviary has an elevated walkway. (p88)

Hong Kong Zoological & Botanical Gardens Look out for the American flamingo, Burmese python and two-toed sloth. (p45)

Kowloon Park Lakes with waterfowl, two playgrounds, swimming pools, an aviary and dragon dances on Sundays. (p130)

Best Activities

Dolphin-watching Hong Kong Dolphinwatch runs four-hour tours to see the native bubble-gum-pink Chinese dolphins. (133)

Symphony of Lights Children will be awestruck by the dance of laser beams projected from skyscrapers on both sides of the harbour. (pictured above; p125)

Peak Tram A ride on this gravity-defying funicular above the skyscrapers will evoke squeals of delight. (p44)

Star Ferry Mini-mariners will have a blast spying passing vessels, as they chug across Victoria Harbour. (p36)

Tram Hong Kong's Harry Potter-esque, skinny double-decker trams rattle, clank and sway amid heavy traffic. (p181)

LGBT+ Travel

ALEXANDER_H_SCHULZ / GETTY IMAGES ©

Hong Kong has a small but growing LGBT+ scene and the annual Pride Parade in November now attracts rainbow flag-wavers by the thousands. That said, Hong Kong Chinese society remains fairly conservative.

Steps Towards Equality

In 1991 the Crimes (Amendment) Ordinance removed criminal penalties for homosexual acts between consenting adults over the age of 18. but since then little progress has been made to address issues of discrimination on the grounds of sexual orientation. It is still not common to see LGBT+ couples making displays of affection in public.

In July 2018 there was a landmark ruling by Hong Kong's Court of Final Appeal, stating that the same-sex partner of a British expat should be granted a spousal visa – a move that has given the local LGBT+ community hope that change (and, importantly, greater equality) is on the horizon.

Best LGBT Nightlife

Petticoat Lane Central club with topless bartender hours, drag shows and a friendly crowd. (p64)

Zoo Local vibe for late-night dancing and drinking in Sheung Wan. (p84)

Behind Sophisticated roaming club night. (p64)

Boo Don't expect a quiet drink, do expect to be entertained at this karaoke and DJ bar in Kowloon. (p154)

Boom (www.facebook.com/boombarmacau) Macau's only gay bar has live music, themed nights and occasional go-go dancers.

T:ME (www.time-bar.com) Low-key cocktail lounge in a Central back alley.

Best Resources

Pink Alliance (https://pinkalliance.hk) For information about LGBTIQ+ culture and events in Hong Kong.

Dim Sum Magazine (http://dimsum-hk.com) Hong Kong's first free gay lifestyle magazine covers local lifestyle, news and entertainment.

Travel Gay Asia (www.travelgayasia.com) An excellent resource for listings of LGBT+ bars across Hong Kong.

Four Perfect Days

Day 1

Armed with your prebooked pass, start early at **Tai Kwun** (p54) heritage and arts complex. Then head west down Hollywood Rd checking out antiques shops and **PMQ**'s (p66) local designers. Stop at **Man Mo Temple** (p72) and explore the hip community on **Tai Ping Shan Street** (p75).

Head back to Central, perhaps taking a scenic ride on a vintage tram, to catch the legendary **Peak Tram** (p44) up to **Victoria Peak** (p38). Stunning views of the city will greet you; perhaps tackle one of the trails.

Dedicate the evening to bar-hopping around **Soho** (p56). Don't miss Asian-accented cocktails in **Old Man** (p63) and **Quinary** (p62), perhaps also catching live jazz at **Peel Fresco** (p66).

Day 2

Embrace (manufactured) nature at lovely **Hong Kong Park** (p88), not forgetting to check out the **Museum of Tea Ware** (pictured above; p89), then head over to the **Blue House** (p87) cluster.

Take the **Star Ferry** (p36) to Kowloon. Enjoy the views along **Tsim Sha Tsui East Promenade** (p124) and savour your stroll to the **Museum of History** (p130). Take afternoon tea in style at the **Peninsula** (p134).

Have your fortune told and catch some Cantonese opera at **Temple Street Night Market** (p144), where you can also get dinner. Then it's not too far a hoof to **Horizonte Lounge** (p153) at the Madera Hotel, where awesome urban skyline views await.

Day 3

Head to Aberdeen for a cruise on the lovely **Aberdeen Harbour** (pictured above; p118), before a spot of shopping (for bargain designer furniture and clothing) at Horizon Plaza on the island of **Ap Lei Chau** (p120). Coffee and cakes are available at several of the furniture shops here. If it's a Saturday, book onto a boozy tour of Hong Kong's own brewery, **Young Master** (p114).

Make your way from Aberdeen to **Sai Kung** (p158) after lunch. Check out Sai Kung Town or hop on a ferry at the waterfront to a nearby **beach** (p159) for a late afternoon dip.

After a busy day, head to **Kowloon Taproom** (p137) for local craft beers and good people-watching.

Day 4

Hop on an early boat, or the new bridge shuttle bus, to Macau. Grab a Portuguese egg tart and explore Macau Peninsula's historic centre, including the atmospheric **St Lazarus Church District** (p168), Largo do Senado and **Ruin of the Church of St Paul** (p162).

Lunch on Macanese fare at **Riquexó Cafe** (p172), then head north to the **Guia Fortress and Chapel** (pictured above right; p169) at the highest point on the peninsula. Make your way southeast to Macau's **Museum of Art** (p169).

If time allows, head to lovely Taipa Village and check out the megacasino complexes in **Cotai** (p169), such as City of Dreams and MGM Cotai, before heading back to Hong Kong.

Need to Know

For detailed information, see Survival Guide p177

Currency
Hong Kong dollar (HK$)

Language Spoken
Cantonese, English

Visas
Visas are not required for Brits (up to 180 days), or Australians, Canadians, EU citizens, Israelis, Japanese, New Zealanders and US citizens (up to 90 days).

Money
ATMs are widely available; international debit/credit cards are accepted in most places.

Time
Hong Kong Time (GMT/UTC plus eight hours)

Tipping
Restaurants Most eateries, except very cheap places, impose a 10% to 15% service charge.

Bars and cafes Not expected unless table service is provided, in which case expect 10% to be added to your bill.

Taxis Never expected.

Daily Budget

Budget: Less than HK$800

Guesthouse or dorm bed: HK$180–450

Meals at a *cha chaan tang* (teahouse) or *dai pai dong* (food stall): HK$60–150

Museums (free); night markets (free); horse races (HK$10)

Bus, tram, ferry ticket: HK$2.60–15

Midrange: HK$800–2500

Double room in a hostel or budget hotel: HK$450–1100

Chinese dinner with three dishes: HK$300

Drinks and live music: HK$500

Top End: More than HK$2500

Double room in a boutique or four-star hotel: HK$2200

Dinner at a top Chinese restaurant: from HK$800

Cantonese opera ticket: HK$200

Advance Planning

Two months before Check dates of Chinese festivals; book accommodation, tickets for major shows, and a table at a top restaurant.

One month before Check listings and book tickets for fringe festivals; book nature tours and a table at a popular restaurant.

Two weeks before Book harbour cruises and your Tai Kwun pass; sign up for email alerts from events organisers.

One week before Check the weather forecast.

Arriving in Hong Kong

✈ Hong Kong International Airport

Airport Express MTR (5.54am to 12.48am, HK$110/$115); 'A' buses (6am to 12.30am, HK$19–$45); taxi to Central/Kowloon (HK$370/270).

🚊 Lo Wu and Lok Ma Chau (Shēnzhèn)

MTR train to city centre (from Lo Wu 5.55am to midnight, from Lok Ma Chau 6.38am to 10.55pm; HK$44–$53).

⛴ Hong Kong–Macau Ferry Terminal

MTR train (Sheung Wan) to Central/Kowloon from 6.05am to 12.56am, HK$5 to HK$10; taxi HK$24 to HK$100.

⛴ China Ferry Terminal

Star Ferry to Central from 6.30am to 11.30pm, HK$2.20 to HK$3.70; taxi HK$34 to HK$44.

Getting Around

Ⓜ MTR

The Mass Transit Railway is the quickest way to get to most urban destinations. Most lines run from 6am to just after midnight.

🚌 Bus

Extensive and as efficient as the traffic allows, but can be bewildering for short-term travellers.

⛴ Ferry

Fast and economical, and throw in spectacular harbour views at no extra cost.

🚊 Tram
Run east to west along Hong Kong Island; convenient and great fun if you're not in a hurry.

🚕 Taxi

Cheap compared with Europe and North America. Most taxis are red; green in certain parts of the New Territories; blue on Lantau Island. All run on meter.

🚐 Minibus

Vans with a green or red roof that cover areas not reachable by bus; green are the easiest for travellers to use.

Hong Kong Neighbourhoods

Sheung Wan & Northwest Hong Kong Island (p71)
Echoes of old Hong Kong, with traditional shops, sumptuous temples and steep ladder streets.

Central District (p35)
Corporate citadels, colonial relics and massive monuments to consumerism.

Temple Street Night Market ◉

Hong Kong Island: Lan Kwai Fong & Soho (p53)
Art galleries, antique stores, stylish bars and the city's party epicentre, where high-life Hong Kongers come to play.

Star Ferry ◉

Man Mo Temple ◉

Tai Kwun ◉

Victoria Peak ◉

Hong Kong Park ◉

Aberdeen & South Hong Kong Island (p109)
Attractive beaches, a seafront bazaar, sampan cruises and one of Asia's best theme parks.

Trip to Macau (p161)
Fortresses, cathedrals and streets, evoking the style of its former Portuguese masters, mingle with Chinese temples and shrines.

Yau Ma Tei & Mong Kok (p143)

Soak up vibes of old Hong Kong in this mosaic of neon and night markets, or explore Mong Kok's sardine-packed commercialism.

Tsim Sha Tsui (p123)

Marvellous museums, an unbeatable harbour setting and all the superlatives Central has to offer on a more human scale.

Tsim Sha
Tsui East
Promenade

Wan Chai, Admiralty & Causeway Bay (p87)

Wan Chai buzzes with markets, nightlife and restaurants, Admiralty boasts stellar views and Causeway Bay is a shopper's dream.

Explore
Hong Kong

Street market, Mong Kok (p146) D3SIGN / GETTY IMAGES ©

Explore

Central District

The minted heart of Asia's financial hub is crammed with corporate citadels, colonial relics and massive monuments to consumerism. It's where you'll find the stock exchange, the Mandarin Oriental, Prada and world-class restaurants and bars, all flaunting their stuff beside the harbour and beneath the gaze of Victoria Peak.

The Short List

○ **Star Ferry (p36)** *Cruising on the iconic green-and-white ferries, the midcentury vessels that cross Victoria Harbour all day and into the night*

○ **HSBC Building (p44)** *Getting up close and personal with a 1980s architectural marvel*

○ **Peak Tram (p44)** *Taking the white-knuckle ascent to Victoria Peak on the Peak Tram for views and strolls around the summit*

○ **Yat Lok (p46)** *Chowing down on dirt-cheap Michelin-starred roast goose*

Getting There & Around

Ⓜ Central station on the Island and Tsuen Wan lines.

🚌 Handy for trying to get to places in between MTR stations and only costs HK$2.60 per ride (Octopus or exact change only).

🚋 Peak Tram runs from the lower terminus (33 Garden Rd) to the Peak.

Neighbourhood Map on p42

HSBC Building interior (p44) RODNEY HYETT / GETTY IMAGES ©

Top Sight 📷
Star Ferry

You can't say you've 'done' Hong Kong until you've taken a ride on a Star Ferry, that legendary fleet of electric-diesel vessels with names such as Morning Star and Twinkling Star. At any time of day the ride, with its riveting views of skyscrapers and soaring mountains, is one of the world's best-value cruises.

◎ MAP P42, E2

天星小輪

www.starferry.com.hk

Pier 7, Central

adult HK$2.20-3.70, child HK$1.50-2.20

🕒 every 6-12min, 6.30am-11.30pm

Ⓜ Hong Kong, exit A2

History

The Star Ferry was founded in 1888 by Dorabjee Nowrojee, a Parsee from Bombay. At the time, most locals were crossing the harbour on sampans. Nowrojee bought a steamboat for his private use, and this eventually became the first Star Ferry. Parsees believe in the Persian religion of Zoroastrianism, and the five-pointed star on the Star Ferry logo is an ancient Zoroastrian symbol.

The Star Ferry features prominently in Hong Kong's history. On Christmas Day 1941, the colonial governor Sir Mark Aitchison Young took the ferry to Tsim Sha Tsui (TST), where he surrendered to the Japanese at the Peninsula. In 1966 thousands gathered at the Tsim Sha Tsui pier to protest against a proposed 5¢ fare increase. The riot that ensued is seen as the trailblazer of local social protests leading to colonial reforms.

The pier you see on Hong Kong Island is an Edwardian replica that replaced the old pier (late-art deco style with a clock tower) at Edinburgh Pl that was demolished despite vehement opposition from Hong Kong people. The Kowloon pier remains untouched.

How to Ride

Take your first trip on a clear night from Tsim Sha Tsui to Central. It's less dramatic in the opposite direction. The lower deck (only open on the Tsim Sha Tsui–Central route) costs a few cents less but gets the full thrust of the ferry's engine noise and diesel fumes.

At the end of the 10-minute journey, watch as a crew member at the back of the boat casts a hemp rope to his colleague who catches it with a billhook, the way it was done in 1880 when the first boat docked.

The Star Ferry operates on two routes – Tsim Sha Tsui–Central and Tsim Sha Tsui–Wan Chai. The first is more popular. Get tickets at the piers.

★ Top Tips

o Snag a seat on the right side of the ferry when headed to TST for the best views.

o The upper deck is well worth the extra few cents, for better views and fewer fumes in your face.

o If you get on the ferry from TST to Hong Kong just after 8pm you'll get front row seats to the nightly Symphony of Lights light show; sit on the left.

✕ Take a Break

Fill up on dim sum at Tim Ho Wan (p48) before or after your (five-minute) voyage.

Relax with a brew at Beer Bay (p50) and watch the ferries come and go.

Top Sight 📷
Victoria Peak

Standing at 552m, Victoria Peak is the highest point on Hong Kong Island. It is also one of the most visited spots by tourists, and it's not hard to see why. Sweeping views of the metropolis, verdant woods, easy but spectacular walks – all reachable in just eight minutes from Central by Hong Kong's earliest form of transport.

◎ MAP P42, B8

維多利亞山頂

www.thepeak.com.hk

Peak Tram Sky Pass adult/child return HK$99/47, adult/child single HK$84/38

🚍15 from Central, below Exchange Sq, 🚋Peak Tram Lower Terminus

Exploring the Peak

Predictably, the Peak has become a money-making circus with restaurants, two shopping malls and various entertainment businesses, but there's still magic up here if you can get past that. Make the pilgrimage up to the Sky Terrace 428 – so named because it stands at 428m above sea level – for the 360-degree views and perfect photo op, but leave time for further exploration.

Secret Garden

Some 500m to the northwest of the upper terminus, up steep Mt Austin Rd, is the site of the old governor's summer lodge, which was burned to the ground by Japanese soldiers during WWII. The stately gatehouse and beautiful gardens remain, however, and have been refurbished with faux-Victorian gazebos and stone pillars. They are open to the public; it takes about 30 minutes to get up here and your reward is that it's blissfully peaceful. Head past the gardens and you'll find a second lookout point with island and sea views.

Hikes

The dappled Morning Trail, a recommended 3.5km circuit of the Peak that takes at least an hour to complete, starts from Peak Galleria heading north up Lugard Rd. It's also possible to hike to Pok Fu Lam Reservoir or descend to Central via two different paths, one which passes through the Zoological & Botanical Gardens and another that follows the Tramway Path. The 50km **Hong Kong Trail** (港島徑) also starts on the Peak. The **Hong Kong Tourist Board Centre** (港島旅客諮詢及服務中心; www.discoverhongkong.com; Peak Piazza, The Peak; ⏱11am-8pm; Peak Tram) in the vintage tram beside the Peak Tower has maps, or download the free Easy Hiking Hong Kong app.

★ Top Tips

○ Avoid paying the Sky Terrace 428 fee and try the charming Lions View Point Pavilion.

○ When the Peak Tram is crazy busy (weekends and public holidays), bus 15 is a good alternative – it's also much cheaper.

○ Pay for the Peak Tram with Octopus to avoid long queues; you can buy the Sky Terrace 428 ticket separately at the top for only HK$5 more than the combined ticket price available at the lower terminus.

○ Bottled water and soft drinks cost up to twice the price on the Peak; bring your own.

✕ Take a Break

Grab a bite at the Peak Lookout (p49), a decent international restaurant in a vintage building.

There are several ice-cream stores by the Peak Tram terminus; grab a cone and sit in the Lions View Point Pavilion's Chinese pagoda with elderly locals.

Walking Tour 🚶

Exploring Hong Kong's Heart

Central has few top museums but it is an area packed with history. It was close to here that the British planted their flag in 1841, it was here that the city's 19th-century port flourished, and it's here that you'll find the biggest concentration of Hong Kong's colonial relics, crouching beneath waves of skyscrapers climbing uphill towards Victoria Peak.

Walk Facts

Start Statue Sq, Central

End Central MTR Station

Length 1.5km; one hour

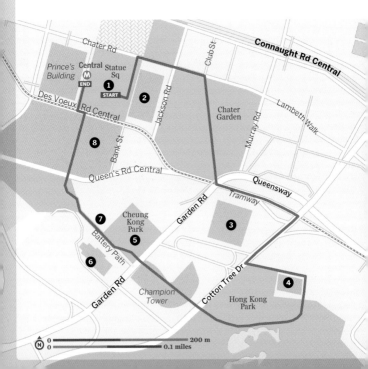

❶ Statue Square

This broad **square** (皇后像廣場; Edinburgh Pl) is a good place to see Hong Kong life congregate – particularly on Sundays when Filipino domestic workers on their day off take over the space, playing cards, chatting over lunch, dancing and singing karaoke.

❷ Old Supreme Court

Next door, the neoclassical **Old Supreme Court Building** (前立法會大樓; 8 Jackson Rd), c 1912, is one of the few colonial-era survivors in the area. During WWII it was a headquarters of the Gendarmerie, the Japanese version of the Gestapo, and many people were executed here.

❸ Bank of China

Walk southwest through Chater Garden and cross Queensway to the angular 70-storey **Bank of China Tower** (中銀大廈; 1 Garden Rd), designed by IM Pei and guarded by sculptures. Some geomancers believe its four prisms are negative symbols; being the opposite of circles, these triangles contradict what circles suggest – money, union and perfection.

❹ Flagstaff House Museum of Tea Ware

Head east into Hong Kong Park for the free Flagstaff House Museum of Tea Ware (p95), displaying valuable pots, cups and other elegant teaware. Sample some of China's finest teas in the serene teahouse next door.

❺ Cheung Kong Park

Stroll west through the park to take elevated walkways over Cotton Tree Dr to hidden Cheung Kong Park, where the tips of the HSBC Building and Bank of China Tower peek through. An artificial waterfall and faux grottoes make it a popular retreat for lunching office workers.

❻ St John's Cathedral

Services have been held at this Anglican **cathedral** (聖約翰座堂; www.stjohnscathedral.org.hk; 4-8 Garden Rd) since it opened in 1849, with the exception of 1944, when the Japanese army used it as a social club. Now dwarfed by skyscrapers, it remains an important historic Hong Kong monument and has unusual features inside, including stained-glass depictions of Hong Kong life.

❼ Former French Mission Building

Follow Battery Path to this handsome **red-brick building** (前法國外方傳道會大樓; 1 Battery Path), built in the mid-1800s and renovated to its current Edwardian glory in 1917 by the French Society of Foreign Missions. It lies empty; admire it from the outside.

❽ HSBC Building

Take the steps down to Queen's Rd Central to the HSBC Building (p44), Central's most famous skyscraper. The bronze lions guarding the harbourside entrance – Stephen (left) and Stitt (right) – predate the building and bear shrapnel scars from the Battle of Hong Kong.

Central District

VICTORIA HARBOUR

For reviews see

◉	Top Sights	p36
◎	Sights	p44
✖	Eating	p46
🍷	Drinking	p50
🛍	Shopping	p51

Pier 1
Pier 2
Pier 3
Pier 4
Pier 5
Pier 6
Pier 7
Pier 8
Pier 9

Government Pier

Ferries to Lamma
Ferries to Cheung Chau
Ferries to Lautau & Peng Chau

Star Ferry

Hong Kong Maritime Museum
◎ 3

Aqua Luna
Pier 10

Man Chiu St
Man Po St
Man Kwong St

24 🍷

Central Pier Bus Terminal

Man Yiu St

Lung Wo Rd

Four Seasons Hotel
✖ 21

IFC Mall
✖ 15

Finance St

Hong Kong (Airport Express Station) Ⓜ
Harbour View St

CENTRAL

Exchange Square
6 ◎

Man Yiu St
Connaught Pl

Connaught Garden

Edinburgh Pl

Queen's Pier

Memorial Gardens

Pier Rd

One IFC

Des Voeux Rd Central

Connaught Rd Central

Gilman St
Jubilee St

Wing Lok St

✖ 16

SHEUNG WAN

Ⓜ Sheung Wan

Queen's Rd Central

Wellington St
Graham St
Peel St
Gough St
Elgin St
Hollywood Rd

13 ✖
✖ 10
Aberdeen St
✖ 14

26 🍷
25
12
11
17
Stanley St
19 ✖
7 🍷

Wellington St Market
8 ◎
9 ◎ 4
18 ✖
Lyndhurst Tce

Victoria St
Man Wa La
Pottinger St
Li Yuen St West
Li Yuen St East
Queen's Rd Central
Chiu Lung St
Stanley St

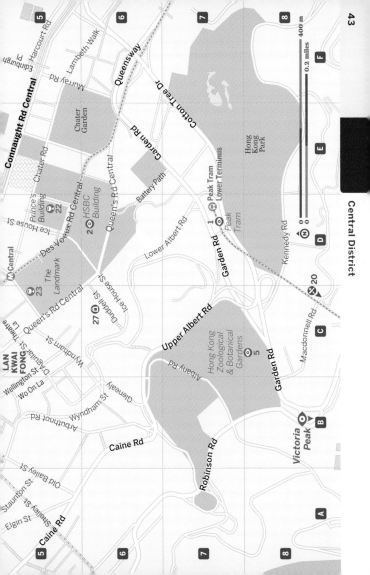

Central District

Sights

Peak Tram
FUNICULAR

1 ◎ MAP P42, D7

This cable-hauled funicular railway has been scaling the 396m ascent to the highest point on Hong Kong Island since 1888. A ride on this clanking tram is a classic Hong Kong experience, with vertiginous views over the city as you ascend up the steep mountainside. It's become so popular in recent years that plans are afoot to move the terminal further up the hill, to better accommodate ever-growing queues that have become a public nuisance at peak times. (☑852 2522 0922; www.thepeak.com.hk; Lower Terminus, 33 Garden Rd, Central; one-way/return adult HK$37/52, child 3-11yr & senior over 65yr HK$14/23; ☺7am-midnight; Ⓜ Central, exit J2)

HSBC Building
NOTABLE BUILDING

2 ◎ MAP P42, D6

This unique building, designed by British architect Sir Norman Foster in 1985, has stood the test of time – more than 30 years on, its magnetism can still be felt in Central. On completion it was the world's most expensive building and considered an engineering marvel, reflecting Foster's wish to break the mould of previous bank architecture. The ground floor is an inviting two-storey walk-through public space, housing an exhibition of HSBC's Hong Kong history and architecture. (滙豐銀行總行大廈; www.hsbc.com.hk/1/2/about/home/unique-headquarters; 1 Queen's Rd, Central; admission free; ☺escalator 9am-4.30pm Mon-Fri, to 12.30pm Sat; Ⓜ Central, exit K)

Hong Kong Maritime Museum
MUSEUM

3 ◎ MAP P42, F2

This multilayered museum records 2000 years of Chinese maritime history and the development of the Port of Hong Kong. Exhibits include ceramics from China's ancient sea trade, shipwreck treasures and old nautical instruments. Modern displays on topics such as diving and conservation are on the upper levels; some of the most eye-opening artefacts are in the basement galleries dedicated to the Canton Trade, including a replica of the first junk to make it to New York in 1847. (香港海事博物館; ☑852 3713 2500; www.hkmaritimemuseum.org; Central Ferry Pier 8, Central; adult/child & senior HK$30/15; ☺9.30am-5.30pm Mon-Fri, 10am-7pm Sat & Sun; ♿; Ⓜ Hong Kong, exit A2)

Graham Street Market
MARKET

4 ◎ MAP P42, A4

This busy street market has been providing Central Hong Kong with fruit, veggies, tofu, duck eggs and all variety of fermented beans and sauces for nearly 200 years. Graham St has been in peril for some years, but urban authority' plans to replace it with hotels and apartments are moving extremely slowly and, for now, this remains one of the most convenient places to see Hong Kong street life in action. (嘉咸街; Graham St, Central; ⏰8am-6pm; 🚌5B)

Hong Kong Zoological & Botanical Gardens

PARK

5 ◉ MAP P42, C8

This Victorian-era garden has a welcoming collection of fountains, sculptures and greenhouses, plus a zoo and some fabulous aviaries. Some 160 species of bird reside here. The small zoo has a collection of monkeys, sloths, lemurs and orangutans, all in a leafy setting. Albany Rd divides the gardens, with the plants and aviaries to the east, close to Garden Rd, and most of the animals to the west. (香港

動植物公園; www.lcsd.gov.hk; Albany Rd, Central; admission free; ⏰terrace gardens 5am-10pm, greenhouse 9am-4.30pm; 🚻; 🚌3B, 12)

Exchange Square

SCULPTURE

6 ◉ MAP P42, D4

This complex of office towers houses the Hong Kong Stock Exchange but what comes as a complete surprise in Central's urban forest is the attractive, elevated sculpture garden at its heart. Here water buffalo graze amid fountains and giant stylised taichi masters tower above lunching office workers. The sculptures are by acclaimed British, Běijīng and Taiwanese artists – Henry Moore, Lynn Chadwick, Ren Zhe and Ju Ming. Access is via a network of overhead walkways linked

Peak Tram

Harbour Tours

The easiest way to see the full extent of Victoria Harbour from sea level is to join an hour-long circular Star Ferry Harbour Tour (p36), of which there are a number of different options (including a daily Symphony of Lights departure). Most of the tours pick up from the Star Ferry Piers in Central, Tsim Sha Tsui and Wan Chai; buy tickets at the pier.

Some other operators offer tours with drinks, nibbles or even buffet dinners. **Aqua Luna** (Map p42, F3; ☏852 2116 8821; www.aqualuna.com.hk; Central Pier 9, Central; from HK$160) runs highly recommended cruises on a traditional Chinese wooden junk boat, with comfy deck seating. Tickets can often be booked on the day, but plan a day or two ahead if you can.

to **IFC Mall** (☏852 2295 3308; www.ifc.com.hk; 8 Finance St, Central; Ⓜ Hong Kong, exit F). (交易廣場; 8 Connaught Pl, Central; Ⓜ Central, exit A)

Eating

Yat Lok   CHINESE $

7 MAP P42, B4

Be prepared to bump elbows with locals at this tiny, basic joint known for its roast goose. Anthony Bourdain gushed over the bird. The leg is the most prized cut and the general rule is the more you pay, the better your meat will be – meals, including rice or slippery noodles, start at HK$56 and rise to HK$170. (一樂燒鵝; ☏852 2524 3882; 34-38 Stanley St, Central; meals HK$56-180; ⏰10am-9pm Thu-Tue, to 5.30pm Sun; Ⓜ Central, exit D2)

Lan Fong Yuen   CAFE $

8 MAP P42, B4

This rickety facade hides an entire *cha chaan tang* (teahouse). Lan Fong Yuen (1952) is believed to be the inventor of the 'pantyhose' milk tea and droves of Instagrammers come to worship here, drink in hand. Over a thousand cups of the strong and silky brew are sold daily alongside pork-chop buns, instant noodles and other delicious hasty tasties. (蘭芳園; ☏852 2854 0731, 852 2544 3895; 2 & 4A Gage St, Central; meals from HK$60, minimum spend HK$28; ⏰7am-6pm Mon-Sat; 🚇5B)

Tai Cheong Bakery   BAKERY $

9 MAP P42, A4

Tai Cheong was best known for its lighter-than-air beignets (deep-fried dough rolled in sugar; *sa yung* in Cantonese) until former governor Chris Patten was photographed wolfing down its egg-custard tarts. Since then 'Fat Patten' egg tarts have hogged the limelight – the buttery BBQ-pork pastries are just as wonderful; frankly it's all delicious. (泰昌餅家; 📞852 3960 6262; 35 Lyndhurst Tce, Central; pastries from HK$6; ⏰8am-8.30pm; 🚇40M)

Kau Kee Restaurant NOODLES $

10 ❌ MAP P42, A3

You can argue till the noodles go soggy about whether Kau Kee has the best beef brisket in town. Whatever the verdict, the meat – served with toothsome noodles in a fragrant beefy broth – is hard to beat. During the 90 years of the shop's existence, film stars and politicians have joined the queue for a table.

Besides regular brisket, you can order – and many of the locals do – the beef tendon (牛筋; *ngau gun*) served in a curry sauce. But know that the best cuts of meat are reserved for the classic dish. (九記牛腩; 📞852 2850 5967; 21 Gough St, Central; meals from HK$50; ⏰12.30-10.30pm Mon-Sat; 🚇Sheung Wan, exit E2)

Butao Ramen JAPANESE $

11 ❌ MAP P42, B4

From the line of customers waiting out front, you can believe that this joint serves the best ramen in town. Choose from the signature Butao with rich pork broth, the spicy Red King, the fusion-y parmesan-enhanced Green King, or the squid-inky Black King. You can also customise how long the noodles should be cooked and the intensity of the broth. (豚王; 📞852 3189 1200; www.butaoramen. com; 69 Wellington St, Central; ramen from HK$89; ⏰11am-11pm; 🚇Central, exit D2)

Mak's Noodle NOODLES, CANTONESE $

12 ❌ MAP P42, B4

Mak's founder emigrated to Hong Kong from China in WWII and established this now-legendary noodle stop, first as a *dai pai dong* (food stall) and then a shop – although now a chain, this Central branch with small street-facing kitchen is the original. Green 1920s chinoiserie decor makes it feel more restaurant-like than its competitors. Try the shrimp wonton soup with beef brisket. (麥奀雲吞麵家; 📞852 2854 3810; www.maksnoodle.sg; 77 Wellington St, Central; noodles from HK$42; ⏰11am-9pm; 🚇Central, exit D2)

Rōnin JAPANESE $$$

13 ❌ MAP P42, A3

With just 24 counter seats locked down behind an unmarked door, Rōnin has all the hallmarks of a coveted Soho dining spot before you've even seen the daily changing menu. Plates – all delicious and inventive – are organised by raw, smaller and bigger, and include revelations like succulent black-pilsner-battered smoked tilefish and crunchy palm-sized crabs with *yuzu* and sesame.

Ask the staff to recommend sake or shochu from the extensive menu to pair with your meal; they really know their stuff. (📞852 2547 5263; www.roninhk.com; Ground fl, 8 On Wo Lane, Central; meals from HK$500; 🕐6pm-midnight Mon-Sat; 📶; Ⓜ Sheung Wan, exit E2)

Lin Heung Tea House

CANTONESE, DIM SUM $

14 🗺 MAP P42, A3

In the morning, this famous 1950s teahouse is packed with older men reading newspapers. Eating here can be overwhelming for the uninitiated: dim sum (from HK$15) is served from trolleys and servers are swamped with locals frantically waving order sheets as soon as they emerge from the kitchen. Little English is spoken; hover near the kitchen if you want to eat. (📞852 2544 4556; Ground fl, 160-164 Wellington St, Central; meals from HK$60; 🕐6am-10pm, dim sum to 3.30pm; Ⓜ Sheung Wan, exit E2)

Tim Ho Wan

DIM SUM $

15 🗺 MAP P42, D3

Opened by a former Four Seasons chef, Tim Ho Wan was the first-ever budget dim sum place to receive a Michelin star. Many relocations and branches later, this iteration beneath IFC Mall may be bland-looking but the star is still tucked snugly inside its tasty titbits (the shrimp dumplings are excellent). Expect to wait 15 to 40 minutes for a seat. (添好運點心專門店; 📞852 2332 3078; www.timhowan.com; Shop 12A, Level 1, Hong Kong Station, Central; meals HK$100-150; 🕐9am-8.30pm; Ⓜ Hong Kong, exit E1)

Yum Cha – Central

DIM SUM $

16 🗺 MAP P42, B2

With four branches across Hong Kong, Yum Cha is one of Hong Kong's most loved modern dim sum chains. Why? Mainly thanks to the super Instagrammable (and admittedly gimmicky) pork buns that look like pigs, and gooey custard buns with eyes. Themed dishes accompany a mix of traditional and twist-on-the-classic dim sum offerings, served with a generous selection of tea. (📞852 3708 8081; www.yumchahk.com; 2nd fl, Nan Fung Place, 173 Des Voeux Rd Central, Central; dishes from HK$50; 🕐11.30am-3pm & 6-11pm, happy hour 6-8pm; 📶; Ⓜ Sheung Wan, exit E3)

Mana! Fast Slow Food

VEGAN $

17 🗺 MAP P42, B4

Craving fresh fruit and veggies? Drop by this vegan and raw-food haven that whips up smoothies, salads and flatbreads (available gluten-free). The latter are baked in-shop by the cheerful staff then smothered with organic greens and Mediterranean dips. Besides tasty, guilt-free food, Mana offers a chilled-out vibe that makes you forget its physical smallness and not-so-bohemian prices. (📞852 2851 1611; www.mana.hk; 92 Wellington St, Central; meals HK$100-200; 🕐10am-10pm; 📶🖊; Ⓜ Central, exit D2)

Chifa Dumpling House

FUSION $$

18 MAP P42, A4

Since the mid-19th century there has been a Chinese diaspora in Peru, cooking home cuisine using Peruvian ingredients. This interpretation of Chinese food is what you'll find at retro-styled Chifa. Dumplings like the violet *xiao long bao* (soup dumplings) with beetroot sauce are supposed to be the main event, but there's a lot more to the menu – all tasty and beautifully presented. (☎ 852 2311 1815; www.chifa.hk; Ground fl, 26 Peel St, Central; dinner from HK$300; ⏰ noon-11pm Sun-Thu, to 11.30pm Fri & Sat; 🛜 ✈)

Luk Yu Tea House

CANTONESE $$

19 MAP P42, B4

This gorgeous formal teahouse (c 1933) with original art deco decor was the haunt of opera artists, writers and painters who came to give recitals and discuss the national fate. The food is old-school Cantonese plus a variety of dim sum dumplings. Prices reflect the grand setting: come for the aesthetics, not a good deal on your dinner. (陸羽茶室; ☎ 852 2523 5464; 24-26 Stanley St, Central; meals from HK$200; ⏰ 7am-9.30pm, dim sum to 6pm; ♿; Ⓜ Central, exit D2)

Peak Lookout

INTERNATIONAL, ASIAN $$

20 MAP P42, C8

This 60-year-old colonial establishment has more character than all the other Peak restaurants com-

Eating Out

🍴

Central is packed with Michelin-starred restaurants and not all of them cost the earth – some are even finger-licking Cantonese cheapies. But even if you're not dining *à la Michelin,* book ahead where possible. Try to avoid the lunch time office rush (noon to 2pm) and expect to queue at many of the best no-reservations restaurants and cafes: Hong Kongers love to eat.

bined, and it's the only place to eat up here that's not inside a mall. It's looking a little shabby around the edges these days, but the food is still good – especially the western selections – and the views from the outdoor terrace are worth lingering over. (太平山餐廳; ☎ 852 2849 1000; www.peaklookout.com.hk; 121 Peak Rd, The Peak; meals from HK$200; ⏰ 10.30am-midnight Mon-Thu, to 1am Fri, 8.30am-1am Sat, 8.30am-midnight Sun; 🚍 15, 🚋 Peak Tram)

Duddell's

CANTONESE $$$

Light Cantonese fare is served in riveting spaces enhanced by artwork at this one-Michelin-starred restaurant-gallery (see 26 🔒 Map p42, C6). There's a graceful dining room, marble-tiled '50s salon and leafy terrace; it's a lovely spot to splash out on exquisite dishes such as barbecued Ibérico pork with honey. Style-wise the contemporary setting far outweighs the competition; the sommelier is also excellent. (都爹利會館; ☎852 2525 9191; www.duddells.co; Level 3 & 4 Shanghai Tang Mansion, 1 Duddell St, Central; dim sum from HK$65, lunch from HK$380, dinner HK$500-1000; ☉noon-2.30pm & 6-10.30pm Mon-Sat; ☎; Ⓜ Central, exit G)

Lung King Heen

CANTONESE, DIM SUM $$$

21 ⓧ MAP P42, C2

The world's first Chinese restaurant to receive three Michelin stars still retains them. The Cantonese food, though by no means peerless in Hong Kong, is excellent. The dining experience is a dichotomy: harbour views and impeccable service, combined with a simple setting devoid of the bells and whistles of Four Seasons' other restaurants, and reasonable prices for the quality. (龍景軒; ☎852 3196 8880; www.fourseasons.com/hong-kong; Four Seasons Hotel, 8 Finance St, Central; meal HK$350-700, weekday set lunch HK$640, yum cha degustation HK$1650; ☉noon-2.30pm Mon-Fri, 11.30am-3pm Sat & Sun & 6-10pm daily; ☎; Ⓜ Hong Kong, exit E1)

Drinking

Sevva

COCKTAIL BAR

22 ⓠ MAP P42, D5

If there was a million-dollar view in Hong Kong, it'd be the one from the balcony of flashy Sevva – skyscrapers so close you can see their arteries of steel, with the harbour

and Kowloon in the distance. At night it takes your breath away, but the prices will too – expect to pay a minimum HK$160 for a glass of wine. (☎852 2537 1388; www.sevva. hk; 25th fl, Prince's Bldg, 10 Chater Rd, Central; ☉noon-midnight Mon-Thu, to 2am Fri & Sat; ☎; Ⓜ Central, exit H)

Dr Fern's Gin Parlour

COCKTAIL BAR

23 ⓠ MAP P42, C5

Just what the doctor ordered: lying somewhere between a Victorian hothouse and a scientific lab, Dr Fern's draws on gin's botanical biology for its trippy look. It's hidden behind a 'Waiting Room' door in the basement of the Landmark mall (enter from Pedder St) and it's table service; wait to be greeted by a doctor. Book ahead for the evening. (☎852 2111 9449; Shop B31A, Landmark Atrium, 15 Queen's Rd Central; ☉noon-1am Sun-Thu, to 2am Fri & Sat; ☎; Ⓜ Central, exit G)

Beer Bay

BAR

24 ⓠ MAP P42, C1

Still wearing your sightseeing grubbies and don't feel up to the glam nightspots of Central? Head to this ultralocal open-air beer kiosk at the ferry pier, a favourite of outer-island dwellers looking for a quick tipple before heading home. Grab a pint of local Gweilo craft beer and sit on the concrete steps watching the water; bring your own snacks. (Hong Kong Central Ferry Pier 3, Central; ☉3-11pm

Mon-Thu, 2-11.30pm Fri & Sat, noon-9.30pm Sun; Hong Kong, exit A1, A2)

Good Spring Co
TEAHOUSE

25 MAP P42, B4

This Chinese medicine shop has a counter selling herbal teas – for detoxing, getting rid of water, cooling the body or treating colds. The most popular is the bitter 24-herb tea. There's also the fragrant chrysanthemum infusion. Watch the staff at the back wrapping precious roots and powder prescriptions as you stand and sip your tea alongside local office workers. (春回堂; ✆852 2544 3518; 8 Cochrane St, Central; tea HK$10-35; ⏰9am-7.30pm; Central, exit D2)

Shopping

Kowloon Soy Company
FOOD & DRINKS

26 MAP P42, B4

The shop (c 1917) for artisanal, naturally fermented soy sauce, premier cru yellow-bean sauce (Chinese miso) and other high-quality condiments; it also sells preserved eggs (皮蛋; *pei darn*) and pickled ginger (酸姜; *suen geung*), which are often served together at restaurants. Did you know that preserved eggs, being alkaline, can make young red wines taste fuller-bodied? Just try it. (九龍醬園; ✆852 2544 3695; www.kowloonsoy.com; 9 Graham St, Central; ⏰8.30am-6.15pm Mon-Fri, to 6pm Sat; Central, exit D1)

Clockenflap

The highlight in Hong Kong's live-music calendar is the excellent outdoor music festival known as **Clockenflap** (香港音樂及藝術節; www.clockenflap.com; Central harbourfront; tickets 1-day HK$820-890, 3-day HK$1410; ⏰Nov or Dec). The three-day event rocks out to regional and local live music of a mostly indie variety, and features art installations and pop-ups. Acts that have played the festival include New Order, the Libertines, A$AP and Massive Attack. Stages are set up next to the harbourfront in Central.

Shanghai Tang
CLOTHING, HOMEWARES

27 MAP P42, C6

This elegant four-level store is a local institution, and one of the few places in Central that specialises in luxury Chinese style. It's the place to go if you fancy a body-hugging *qípáo* (cheongsam) with a modern twist, a Chinese-style clutch or a lime-green mandarin jacket. Shanghai Tang also stocks beautiful chinoiserie-style homewares; don't expect to find much below HK$1000. (上海灘; ✆852 2525 7333; www.shanghaitang.com; 1 Duddell St, Shanghai Tang Mansion, Central; ⏰10.30am-8pm; Central, exit D1)

Explore ⊛
Hong Kong Island: Lan Kwai Fong & Soho

Central's raucous bedfellows, Lan Kwai Fong and Soho are where well-heeled Hong Kongers come to play and together they form the party epicentre of Hong Kong. Soho ('south of Hollywood Rd') is also stuffed with art galleries, antique shops and high-end boutiques perfect for treasure hunting.

The Short List

o **Tai Kwun (p54)** *Admiring how art and heritage are cleverly celebrated in this long-awaited reinvention of the old Central Police Station*

o **PMQ (p66)** *Foraging for Hong Kong–designed jewellery, clothes and homewares at this huge heritage site with coffee, cocktails and art*

o **Quinary (p62)** *Witnessing Asian-infused mixology magic at one of the world's best cocktail bars*

Getting There & Around

Ⓜ Central MTR exit D2 is the closest you can get to Lan Kwai Fong and Soho by train; after that it's a sweaty climb.

🚌 Number 26 travels along Hollywood Rd through Soho, linking the area with Central and Sheung Wan.

Central–Mid-Level Escalator Useful for reaching LKF and Soho's uphill bars and restaurants.

Neighbourhood Map on p58

Top Sight 📷
Tai Kwun

Contemporary Swiss design fuses with colonial relics at Tai Kwun, a reimagining of the old Central Police Station and one of Hong Kong Island's most significant preservation projects to date. Renovations took eight years, during which time one of the original blocks even collapsed, but this long-awaited behemoth of a heritage and arts complex finally opened in May 2018.

🎯 MAP P58, C4

📞 852 3559 2600

www.taikwun.hk

10 Hollywood Rd, Lan Kwai Fong

admission free

🕙 10am–11pm, visitor centre to 8pm

Site History

The site was founded in 1841 for the British army when it occupied Hong Kong during the First Opium War. When the Chinese ceded the territory to Britain in 1842 it became the flag-bearer for colonial law and order, and a rare example of a police station, magistracy and prison neatly packaged into one complex. Buildings were added over time up until the early 20th century, and the complex became a declared monument in 1995. Visits should start in the Barrack Block, where the high-tech Main Heritage Gallery explores the site's full history.

Navigating the Grounds

The complex is vast, comprising 16 original blocks and two starkly contrasting new ones, repurposed as a mix of history exhibitions, art galleries, shopping and dining. Info boards stationed around the site tell little-known stories collected from locals and officers who once worked here.

Leave time to linger in the prison cells of B Hall (Block 12), where animated silhouettes of prisoners bring to life the conditions for inmates – including Vietnam revolutionary Ho Chi Minh, who was interred here in the 1930s. And visit the old entranceway to Victoria Prison (off Arbuthnot Rd), which was at some point converted into a makeshift chapel. Its frescoes were discovered beneath white paint during the restoration project and are now being restored.

★ Top Tips

o Register online for the free Tai Kwun Visitors Pass to guarantee entry with an assigned day and time; the site's daily visitor capacity is capped and walk-ins are often not accepted.

o Visit midweek to avoid the crowds, and set aside half a day to see everything.

o Take the popular 45-minute guided heritage tour (book in advance).

✕ Take a Break

Book lunch at Tai Kwun's excellent, Herzog & de Meuron–designed Chinese restaurant, Old Bailey (p60).

Debrief over a drink at Behind Bars (p65), hidden inside a series of interlinking old prison cells in E Hall (Block 15).

Walking Tour 🥾

Lan Kwai Fong Pub Crawl

The beats are on, the drinks are being poured, it's not even dusk: you must be in Lan Kwai Fong. Hong Kong's party epicentre is loud and proud, but many of the best bars in this 'hood are actually up steep stairs or behind unmarked doors. Things get classier as the streets merge into Soho. Drinks are pricey, so start your crawl early and follow the happy hours.

Walk Facts

Start Cé La Vi

End Peel Fresco or Quinary

Length 1km; taking as long as you can last!

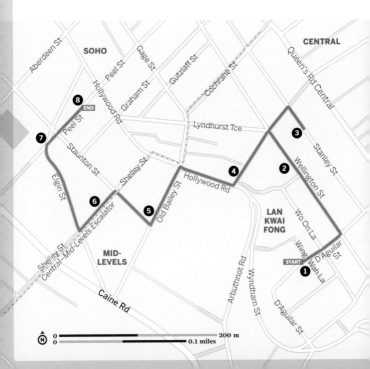

❶ Cé La Vi

The glam rooftop terrace of **Cé La Vi** (http://hk.celavi.com; 25th fl, California Tower, 32 D'Aguilar St) on D'Aguilar St is the place to be in Lan Kwai Fong for sunset, in touching distance of the skyscrapers. Take the elevator to the 25th floor and then keep going up until you reach the open-air Skydeck.

❷ Honi Honi

Back at street level, D'Aguilar St is ground zero for LKF's tackiest bars, so don't stop. Head northwest to retro-chic tiki-bar **Honi Honi** (www.honihonibar.com; 3rd fl, Somptueux Central Bldg, 52 Wellington St) and its secret outdoor patio in the sky. Take advantage of the decent happy hour, when cocktails – made with fresh fruit – start from HK$40.

❸ Yat Lok

Afterwards, detour northwest to Michelin-starred Yat Lok (p46) for roast goose. Little English is spoken, but there's a menu and takeaway is available so you can grab some on the go.

❹ Iron Fairies

Retrace your steps up the ladder street and head up another block to **Iron Fairies** (www.facebook.com/theironfairieshongkong; Lower ground fl, 1-13 Hollywood Rd). This pricey cocktail bar is unlike anything else in Hong Kong. Ten thousand butterflies flutter from copper threads attached to the ceiling, in an underground cave designed to mimic a blacksmith's foundry where tables are piled with fairies forged from iron.

❺ Pontiac

From here, hop up to Hollywood Rd and head west, skirting the colonial-era exterior of Tai Kwun heritage complex on to Old Bailey St. Here you'll find the Pontiac (p64), the friendliest dive bar with LKF's best music and HK$15 beers until 8pm.

❻ Peak Cafe Bar

You'll have to cross the Central–Mid-Level Escalator to get to the welcoming **Peak Cafe Bar** (www.cafedecogroup.com; 9-13 Shelley St), decorated with the charming fixtures and fittings of the old Peak Cafe from 1947. Plant yourself by the window during happy hour and watch commuters glide by.

❼ 65 Peel

A few strides further up Shelley St, turn northwest into Elgin St and continue until you hit 65 Peel (p63) on Peel St. Stop for a beer flight of local craft brews. Then tumble down Peel St until you hit the teeny temple with coiled incense burners at the top of the steps just across Staunton St.

❽ Peel Fresco

Spiritually refreshed, continue down Peel St. Keep your fingers crossed that you hear jazz notes crashing out of Peel Fresco (p66). This intimate live-music bar is a fitting place to end the night.

A   B   C   D

1

SHEUNG WAN

Bonham Strand E

Hillier St

Mercer St

Jervois St

Queen's Rd Central

Kau U Fong

Wing Kut St

Gilman's Bazaar

Des Voeux Rd Central

N   0 ———————————— 200 m
    0 ———————————— 0.1 miles

2   Hollywood Rd

Gough St

Mee Lun St

Aberdeen St

Peel St

Wellington St

Queen's Rd Central

Jubilee St

Queen Victoria St

Shing Wong St

Staunton St

8 ✗
28 ⊕
7 ✗ **17** ✗
26 ⊕ **12** ✗
6 ✗
13 ⊕
Hollywood Rd
Elgin St
22 ✗
23 ☆
24 ⊕

Gage St

Graham St

Gutzlaff St

Stanley St

Cochrane St

1 ⊙
Central-
Mid-Levels
Escalator

3   Caine Rd

Aberdeen St

14 ✗

9 ✗
Staunton St
Graham St

Peel St

Elgin St

SOHO

Lyndhurst Tce

Ezra's La

Iyara

Stanley St

Wellington St

3 ⊙
Dr Sun Yat-Sen
Museum

Shelley St

25 ⊕
Hollywood Rd

21 ✗

4

4 ✗

15 ✗
Old Bailey St

5 ✗

Tai Kwun
⊙

27 ✗

19 ⊕
10 ✗

LAN
KWAI
FONG

Arbuthnot Rd

20 ⊕

11 ⊕
16 ⊕

18 ⊕
Lan Kwai Fong

D'Aguilar St

Wyndham St

Caine Rd

Chancery La

Peel St

Shelley St

2 ⊙
Jamia
Mosque

MID-
LEVELS

Mosque Jct

5

Arbuthnot Rd

Glenealy

Caine Rd

6

Robinson Rd

Upper Albert Rd

Hong Kong
Zoological &
Botanical
Gardens

Glenealy

For reviews see	
⊙ Top Sights	p54
⊙ Sights	p59
✗ Eating	p60
⊕ Drinking	p62
☆ Entertainment	p66
⊕ Shopping	p66

A   B   C   D

Sights

Central–Mid-Levels Escalator

LANDMARK

1 ◉ MAP P58, D2

The world's longest covered outdoor people-mover zigzags from Central's offices to homes near Conduit Rd in the Mid-Levels using an 800m system of escalators and walkways. Embark and watch the streets unveil – do so early evening, heading uphill from where it starts on Queen's Rd Central, and you'll see one of the world's most serene daily commutes. It's also very handy for reaching the bars of Soho without having to sweat and puff your way up the steep ladder streets. (Soho; ◷down 6-10am, up 10.30am-midnight)

Jamia Mosque

MOSQUE

2 ◉ MAP P58, A5

Also called Lascar Mosque after the Indian sea people it was originally built for, Hong Kong's oldest mosque is a mint-green beauty now dwarfed by the Mid-Level high-rises. The first mosque on this site was erected in 1849 and called Mohammedan; the one here today was built in 1915. Non-Muslims can enter on casual guided tours during opening hours, or just drop by to admire its facade from the terrace. Jamia Mosque is accessible from the Central–Mid-Levels Escalator. (些利街清真寺; Lascar Mosque; ☎852 2523 7743, 852 2838 9417; 30 Shelley St, Mid-Levels; ◷tours 11.30am-8pm Tue-Thu, Sat & Sun, 3-8pm Fri)

Central–Mid-Levels Escalator

BENNY MARTY / SHUTTERSTOCK ©

Pampering With a View

Many of Hong Kong's city spas are positively cave-like, in low-lit high-rises with no windows. **Iyara** (Map p58, C3; ☑852 2545 8638; www.iyaradayspa. com; 1st fl, 26 Cochrane St, Lan Kwai Fong; manicure/pedicure from HK$160/250, massage from HK$380; ⏰10am-9pm Mon-Thu, to 8pm Fri & Sat, 11am-8pm Sun), however, is more like a secret garden. It's run by friendly Thais who use organic, natural products. Floor-to-ceiling windows at eye level with the Central–Mid-Level Escalator provide entertainment while getting a manicure or foot massage with a (free) glass of wine.

Dr Sun Yat-Sen Museum   MUSEUM

 3 ◎ MAP P58, A3

Dr Sun Yat-Sen was a key figure in the fight to establish a Chinese republic and served as its first president in the days after the revolution in 1911, later founding the Kuomintang – Chinese Nationalist Party. Housed in a grand Edwardian building, this museum of archival material dedicated to his life is fascinating but confusingly laid out – start on the 2nd floor, which is the best place to learn why Yat-Sen is considered the father of modern China. (孫中山紀念館; ☑852 2367

6373; http://hk.drsunyatsen.museum; 7 Castle Rd, Mid-Levels; admission free; ⏰10am-6pm Mon-Wed & Fri, to 7pm Sat & Sun; 🚍40M)

Eating

Motorino   PIZZA $

4 🍴 MAP P58, B4

This skinny, buzzing outpost of the famed NYC pizzeria puts out charcoal-kissed Neapolitan pizza with a bubbly and flavourful crust that will give your jaws a delectable workout. The brussels-sprout and smoked-pancetta version is especially glorious. Reservations accepted for lunch; the fixed-price weekday lunch menu is a good deal at HK$138 for pizza and a soft drink. (☑852 2801 6881; www.moto rinopizza.com; 14 Shelley St, Soho; meals HK$170-380; ⏰noon-midnight; 🛜♿; Ⓜ Central, exit D2)

Old Bailey   CHINESE $$

5 🍴 MAP P58, C4

The joy of Old Bailey begins with its snazzy Herzog & de Meuron–designed interior that mixes mid-century-modern Scandi with Chinese design principles, and the sweeping outdoor terrace overlooking Tai Kwun and Soho's skyscrapers. The food lives up to its surroundings, with dishes like Longjing-tea-smoked pigeon, pork belly with spindly shimeji mushrooms and juicy *xiao long bao* (soup dumplings) with Sichuan peppercorns. (☑852 2877 8711; www.oldbailey.hk; 2nd fl, JC

Contemporary, Tai Kwun, Old Bailey St, Soho; meals from HK$300; 🕙noon-3pm & 6-11pm Mon-Sat, lounge bar noon-11pm; 🛜🍴; 🚇26)

Little Bao
FUSION $$

6 🍴 MAP P58, A3

A trendy diner that wows with its *bao* (Chinese buns) – snow-white orbs crammed with juicy meat and slathered with Asian condiments – and fusion sharing dishes. Its signature pork-belly *bao* with hoisin ketchup, and truffle fries with shiitake tempeh might just be the greatest, most unusal meal you have in Hong Kong. Go early to put your name on the waiting list – no reservations. (📞852 2194 0202; www.little-bao.com; 66 Staunton St, Sheung Wan; meals HK$200-400; 🕙6-11pm Mon-Fri, noon-4pm & 6-11pm Sat, noon-4pm & 6-10pm Sun; 🛜🍴; 🚇Central, exit D2)

Ho Lee Fook
HONG KONG $$

7 🍴 MAP P58, B3

As irreverent as its name suggests, this buzzy underground spot does a winkingly modern take on retro Chinatown cuisine. Fat prawn toasts are served with Kewpie mayo, the *char siu* uses upmarket Kurobuta pork, and prawn *lo mein* is spangled with crunchy fried garlic and slicked with shellfish oil. It's justifiably popular and the atmosphere is see-and-be-seen, despite nightclub-level darkness. (📞852 2810 0860; http://holeefookhk. tumblr.com; Ground fl, 1-5 Elgin St,

Soho; meals HK$250-500; 🕙6-11pm Sun-Thu, to midnight Fri & Sat; 🛜; 🚇Central, exit D2)

Aberdeen Street Social
BRITISH $$

8 🍴 MAP P58, B2

Run by British celebrity chef Jason Atherton, trendy Aberdeen Street Social is really two restaurants in one. Downstairs is an all-day cafe where hip Sheung Wan dwellers eat avocado toast and fancy fish and chips on the patio. Upstairs is pricey, avant-garde dining (think smoked eel with foie gras). Its lunch deal is a snip compared with usual prices: HK$298 for three courses.

Happy hour runs 5pm to 8pm Sunday to Friday. (📞852 2866 0300; www.aberdeenstreetsocial. hk; Ground fl, PMQ, 25 Aberdeen St, Central; downstairs meals HK$150-300, upstairs meals HK$400-800; 🕙noon-11pm; 🛜; 🚇Sheung Wan)

Chom Chom
VIETNAMESE $$

9 🍴 MAP P58, B3

Wildly popular and always lively, Chom Chom recreates Vietnamese street food with bold flavours and charcoal grills, which are best washed down with its craft beers on tap. The corner location makes for great people-watching and is often crowded with queuers. Pho fans take note: Chom Chom's version is a refreshing noodle roll with beef, baby garlic and Thai basil. (📞852 2810 0850; www. chomchom.hk; 58-60 Peel St, Soho;

Drinking in Hong Kong

It's downright expensive to drink in Hong Kong. An all-night boozy tour can set you back at least HK$800. Thrifty drinkers often buy from convenience stores as there is no law against drinking alcohol in public in Hong Kong. Alternatively, plan your nights around happy-hour hopping, which can halve the cost of drinks.

meals HK$350-500; ⏱5pm-late Sat-Wed, from 6pm Thu-Fri; 🛜; Ⓜ Central, exit D1)

Yung Kee Restaurant
CANTONESE $$

10 🍴 MAP P58, D4

The roast goose here, made from fowl raised in the restaurant's farm and roasted in coal-fired ovens, has been the talk of the town since 1942. It's thanks to the special sauce; a light and aromatic, meaty gravy served with yellow beans marinated in Chinese five spice. Cheaper rice and meat dishes, including the signature goose, are available 2pm to 5.30pm. (鏞記; 📞852 2522 1624; www.yungkee.com.hk; 32-40 Wellington St, Lan Kwai Fong; lunch from HK$150, dinner HK$250-500; ⏱11am-11.30pm; 👶; Ⓜ Central, exit D2)

Carbone
ITALIAN $$$

11 🍴 MAP P58, D5

The only foreign outpost of the over-the-top New York Italian-American joint, Carbone makes you feel like Frank Sinatra having dinner in 1963. Walls are panelled in dark wood, chairs are red leather, waiters rock maroon tuxedos and desserts come on a rolling cart. Retro classics include a bigger-than-your-head veal parmesan and a huge, satisfying tangle of spaghetti and meatballs. (📞852 2593 2593; www.carbone.com.hk; 9th fl, LKF Tower, 33 Wyndham St, Lan Kwai Fong; mains HK$220-600, set lunch for 2 HK$388 per person; ⏱noon-2.30pm Mon-Sat, 6-11.30pm Sun-Thu, to midnight Fri & Sat)

Drinking

Quinary
COCKTAIL BAR

12 🍸 MAP P58, B3

Consistently voted one of the world's top 50 bars, Quinary is a sleek, moodily lit cocktail bar that attracts a well-dressed crowd. Its gifted mixologists create homemade infusions of spirits and the Asian-inspired cocktails are delicious, theatrical marvels. Signature creations include the Quinary Sour (whisky, homemade liquorice syrup, bonito flakes) and the Instagram-killing Earl Grey Caviar Martini with whipped air. (📞852 2851 3223; www.quinary.hk;

56-58 Hollywood Rd, Soho; ⏰5pm-1am Mon-Sat; 📶; Ⓜ Central, exit D2)

Old Man

COCKTAIL BAR

13 🍸 MAP P58, A3

If Ernest Hemingway was still alive today, chances are he'd love this tiny no-sign speakeasy named after his novel *The Old Man and the Sea*, with a neo-cubist portrait of Papa himself looking down approvingly from behind the bar. The atmosphere is friendly rather than pretentious and the mixology is exceptionally creative, with elements like gruyère, sous-vide pandan leaves and nori dust. (📞852 2703 1899; www.theoldmanhk.com; Lower ground fl, 37-39 Aberdeen St, Soho; cocktails HK$100; ⏰5pm-2am Mon-Sat, to midnight Sun; Ⓜ Central, exit D2)

65 Peel

CRAFT BEER

14 🍺 MAP P58, B3

Everything you need to know about Hong Kong's craft-beer scene is on page one of 65 Peel's beer menu, dedicated to local taps from breweries like Young Master, Lion Rock and Moonzen. Beers are listed from 1 to 12 by strength, and bitterness is indicated by the IBU ranking; try a beer flight of four 200mL serves for HK$140.

Quiet during the day, this industrial-style craft-beer bar gets going at night, when its pink-neon wall feature gives the bare-concrete space an eerie glow. There's a food menu of reinvented Hong Kong dishes to line your stomach. (📞852 2342 2224; www.facebook.com/65peel; Ground fl, 65

Old Man cocktail bar

SOUTH CHINA MORNING POST / CONTRIBUTOR / GETTY IMAGES ©

Peel St, Soho; ◷4pm-midnight Mon-Sat, from 2pm Sun; 🛜)

Pontiac
BAR

15 🗺 MAP P58, C4

There's something indescribably comfortable about the Pontiac, which rocks to a different tune to most of the cheesy bars in LKF. It's a skinny, open-fronted, graffiti-covered dive that's wholly run by women, with a string of bras hanging behind the bar to let you know who's in charge. Alternative music, friendly vibe, HK$15 happy-hour beers: what's not to love? (☎852 2521 3855; 13 Old Bailey St, Lan Kwai Fong; ◷5pm-12.30am Mon-Fri, from 3pm Sat, 3-10.30pm Sun, happy hour 5-8pm; 🛜; 🚌26)

Stockton
COCKTAIL BAR

16 🗺 MAP P58, D5

Hard-to-find Stockton evokes the ambience of a private club in Victorian London with Chesterfield sofas and wood panelling cleverly arranged to form dark, intimate corners. Its signature cocktails (from HK$130) are inspired by famous writers and quirkily served in vessels such as ceramic pots with rosemary fronds to garnish. Make a reservation if you're coming after 9pm on a weekend. (☎852 2565 5268; www.stockton.com.hk; 32 Wyndham St, Lan Kwai Fong; ◷6pm-2am Mon-Wed, to 4am Thu-Sat; Ⓜ Central, exit D2)

Club 71
BAR

17 🗺 MAP P58, B3

This friendly, unassuming bar with a bohemian vibe is named after a protest march on 1 July 2003. It's a favourite haunt of local artists and activists who come for cheap beer and jamming sessions. In the public garden out front, revolutionaries plotted to overthrow the Qing dynasty a hundred years ago. Enter from the alley next to 69 Hollywood. (☎852 2858 7071; Basement, 67 Hollywood Rd, Soho; ◷5pm-1am Mon-Sat, happy hour 5-9pm; 🛜; 🚌26, Ⓜ Central, exit D1)

Behind
CLUB

18 🗺 MAP P58, D5

Behind started at one of the first gay clubs in Hong Kong, Club 97 in Lan Kwai Fong (now closed), and has gone on to become a roving club night. It's an inclusive night, popular within the LGBT community but not exclusively so, regularly attracting about 600 people. Venues change every couple of months; check online. (www.facebook.com/clubbehind; 38-44 D'Aguilar St, Central; ◷last Sat of month)

Petticoat Lane
GAY & LESBIAN

19 🗺 MAP P58, D4

Central's best LGBT night out is Petticoat Lane, a basement club with sparkling foliage hanging above the bar, a dance floor, small outdoor terrace and gender-neutral toilets. The vibe is inclusive and its weekly 'Wednesgay' evenings with topless bartenders include free-flow Absolut vodka (10pm to 11pm) for all and sundry. There's a drag show every night at midnight. (📞852 2808 2738; www. petticoatlane.club; Basement, 57-59 Wyndham St, Lan Kwai Fong; 🕐6pm-2am Tue & Thu, to 3am Wed, to 4am Fri, 8pm-4am Sat; Ⓜ Central, exit D2)

Behind Bars   BAR

20 🚇 MAP P58, C4

A series of interlinking jail cells in the former Central Police Station, now Tai Kwun (p54) heritage complex, have been given a clever makeover to create this quirky bar. Inside red-brick 'Block 15', the whitewashed cells now have mirrored walls and nooks to sit in, while a communal table fills the central aisle where wardens would have once paced. (www.facebook. com/behindbars.hk; E-Hall, Tai Kwun, Arbuthnot Rd, Soho; 🕐4pm-midnight Tue-Sun; 🚌26)

Slide on 79   SPORTS BAR

21 🚇 MAP P58, D4

If you're looking for sports screens but reluctant to set foot in a mock English or Irish pub, Slide on 79 has you covered. But with its cocktail menu, live gigs, mural wall and pleasant open frontage in the middle of LKF, it's a good spot any time – this is far from your average sports bar. Enter from Pottinger St. (📞852 2779 9279; www.slideon79.

What's On & Tickets

Urbtix (📞ticketing enquiries 10am-8pm 852 3761 6661; www. urbtix.hk) and **Hong Kong Ticketing** (📞ticket hotline 10am-8pm 852 3128 8288; www. hkticketing.com) have tickets to every major event in Hong Kong. You can book through them or purchase tickets at the performance venues; Urbtix tickets can be collected from a handful of kiosks around town.

com; Harilela House, 79 Wyndham St, Lan Kwai Fong; 🕐11.45am-midnight Mon & Tue, to 1am Wed & Thu, to 3am Fri & Sat, 3pm-12.30am Sun, happy hour 3-8pm; 📶)

Kung Lee   JUICE BAR

22 🚇 MAP P58, B3

This institution in the heart of Soho has been quietly selling herbal teas and fresh sugar-cane juice since 1948 – its quality is unchanged, as are the charming vintage tiles, posters and signs. There's 'turtle jelly' too, made with the powdered shell of a certain type of turtle and a variety of Chinese herbs. It's good for cooling and detoxing. (公利真料竹蔗水; 📞852 2544 3571; 60 Hollywood Rd, Soho; juice from HK$14; 🕐11am-10pm; 🚌26)

PMQ:
Heritage Reinvented

This arts and lifestyle **hub** (元創方; ☎852 2870 2335; www.pmq.org.hk; S614, Block A, PMQ, 35 Aberdeen St, Soho; ⏱building 7am-11pm, shops noon-8pm; 🚌26, Ⓜ Central, exit D2) occupies the multistorey modernist building complex of the old married police quarters (c 1951). Dozens of small galleries and shops, including a branch of G.O.D., hawk local design in the form of hip handmade jewellery, clothing, housewares and more, making the PMQ a terrific place to hunt for nontacky souvenirs. There are also several restaurants and cafes, a breezy central courtyard hosting pop-ups and street art, and a large space on the top floor with rotating free exhibitions.

The site's earliest incarnation was a temple built in 1843, which was subsequently replaced by Central School, where Nationalist leader Dr Sun Yatsen once studied. Remnants of the school remain. PMQ is bounded by Hollywood Rd (north), Staunton St (south), Aberdeen St (east) and Shing Wong St (west).

Entertainment

Peel Fresco   JAZZ

23 ⭐ MAP P58, B3

Charming Peel Fresco has live jazz six nights a week, with local and overseas acts on an intimate stage close enough for listeners to chink glasses with musicians. It's small, relaxed and friendly, and there's no better place in Soho than here curled up with a drink when the action starts around 9.30pm; come at 9pm to secure a seat. (☎852 2540 2046; www.peelfresco.com; 49 Peel St, Soho; ⏱5.30pm-late Tue-Sun; 🚌13, 26, 40M)

Shopping

G.O.D.   GIFTS, HOUSEWARES

24 🔒 MAP P58, B3

Goods of Desire – or G.O.D. – is a cheeky local lifestyle brand, selling homewares, clothes, books and gifts with retro Hong Kong themes. Fun buys include aprons printed with images of Hong Kong's famous neon signs, bed linen with themes like koi fish, and reasonably priced cheongsam tops in modern fabrics and colours; great for souvenirs. There's another branch in **PMQ**. (Goods of Desire; ☎852 2805 1876; www.god.com.hk; 48 Hollywood Rd, Soho; ⏱11am-9pm)

Wattis Fine Art

ANTIQUES

25 🔒 MAP P58, C4

This upstairs gallery has an outstanding collection of antique maps, lithographs, photos and posters for sale. Rarely will you find such an extensive homage to Asian history, covering not just Hong Kong and Macau, but also Chinese cities like Shànghǎi and Southeast Asian destinations such as Borneo, Myanmar (Burma), Malaka and Mumbai. Enter from Old Bailey St. (www.wattis.com.hk; 2nd fl, 20 Hollywood Rd, Lan Kwai Fong; ⊙10.30am-6pm Mon-Sat; 🚇26)

Soul Art

ARTS & CRAFTS

26 🔒 MAP P58, B3

This Běijīng import brings traditional Chinese culture to life in the form of handmade polymer clay and cloth figurines – and it's actually a lot cooler and more beautiful than it sounds. The dainty baskets of rainbow-coloured dumplings and cloth tigers hand-stitched and hand-painted with peonies are both adorable – as is the shop's fluffy ginger cat, Tiger. (☎852 2857 7786; www.soulartshop.com; Ground fl, 24-26 Aberdeen St, Soho; ⊙11am-8pm; 🚇26)

Mountain Folkcraft

GIFTS & SOUVENIRS

27 🔒 MAP P58, D4

This is one of the nicest shops in the city for folk craft, and one of the most reasonably priced for vintage Asian artefacts. It's piled with bolts of batik and sarongs, clothing, wood carvings, lacquerware and paper cuts made by ethnic minorities in China and other Asian countries. (高山民藝; ☎852 2523 2817; www.mountainfolkcraft.com; 12 Wo On Lane, Lan Kwai Fong; ⊙10am-6.30pm Mon-Sat; Ⓜ Central, exit C)

Arch Angel Antiques

ANTIQUES

28 🔒 MAP P58, B3

Though the specialities are ancient porcelain and tombware, Arch Angel packs a lot more into its two floors: it has everything from old ink drawings and terracotta horses to palatial furniture, with friendly staff to help you navigate the well-displayed stock. Prices range from about HK$3000 to HK$1 million. (☎852 2851 6848; 70 Hollywood Rd, Lan Kwai Fong; ⊙9.30am-6.30pm Mon-Sat, to 6pm Sun; 🚇26)

Worth a Trip 👀
Po Lin Monastery & Big Buddha

No trip to Hong Kong is complete without visiting Ngong Ping Plateau for the seated Tian Tan Buddha statue, the biggest of its kind in the world. It can be seen aerially as you fly into Hong Kong, or on a clear day from Macau, but nothing beats coming up close and personal with this much-loved spiritual icon over 500m up in the western hills of Lantau.

寶蓮禪寺

📞 852 2985 5248

🕐 9am-6pm

Ⓜ Tung Chung

⛴ Outlying Islands Terminal, Central Pier 6 to Mui Wo, Lantau Island

🚌 2 from Mui Wo, 23 from Tung Chung

Tian Tan Buddha

Commonly known as the 'Big Buddha', the Tian Tan Buddha (pictured left) is a representation of Lord Gautama some 23m high, or just under 34m if you include the lotus and podium. It was unveiled in 1993, and still holds the honour as the tallest seated bronze Buddha statue in the world. It's well worth climbing the 268 steps for the views and a closer look. The Buddha's birthday, a public holiday in April or May, is a lively time to visit when thousands make the pilgrimage. Visitors are requested to observe some decorum in dress and behaviour. It is forbidden to bring meat or alcohol into the grounds.

On the second level of the podium is a small **museum** containing oil paintings and ceramic plaques of the Buddha's life and teachings.

Po Lin Monastery

Po Lin Monastery, a huge Buddhist complex built in 1924, is more of a tourist honeypot than a religious retreat, attracting hundreds of thousands of visitors a year, and it's still being expanded. Most of the buildings you'll see on arrival are new, with the older, simpler ones tucked away behind them. Po Lin Vegetarian Restaurant in the monastery is famed for its inexpensive but filling vegetarian food.

Ngong Ping 360 Cable Car

The most spectacular way to get to the plateau is by the 5.7km **Ngong Ping 360** (昂平360纜車; www.np360.com.hk; adult/child/concession one-way from HK$145/70/95, return from HK$210/100/140; �》10am-6pm Mon-Fri, 9am-6.30pm Sat, Sun & public holidays; 👪), a cable car linking Ngong Ping with the centre of Tung Chung (downhill and to the north). The journey over the bay and the mountains takes 25 minutes, with each glassed-in gondola carrying 17 passengers. The upper station is at the skippable theme park–like Ngong Ping Village just west of the monastery.

★ Top Tips

o Book your cable-car tickets online in advance to avoid some of the wait.

o The glass-bottomed Crystal Cabin is well worth the extra HK$80, plus it has shorter lines.

o If the wait for the cable cars is too long, consider taking the bus up and riding the cable car down. Return lines are always shorter.

✗ Take a Break

o The monastery's **Po Lin Vegetarian** (寶蓮禪寺齋堂; ☎852 2985 5248; Ngong Ping; set meals regular/deluxe HK$110/150; ☸11.30am-4.30pm; ♪) restaurant serves meat-free Buddhist cuisine.

o To the left of the monastery, a small snack shop sells lovely handmade sweets – try the mango dumplings or fried sesame balls.

Worth a Trip g Po Lin Monastery & Big Buddha

Explore

Sheung Wan & Northwest Hong Kong Island

At the foot of Victoria Peak, Sheung Wan carries the echo of 'Old Hong Kong', with its traditional shops, delicious temples and steep 'ladder streets', composed entirely of stairs. Stretching further west, the charming neighbourhoods of Sai Ying Pun and Kennedy Town still offer a generous slice of local life.

The Short List

○ **Man Mo Temple (p72)** *Breathing in the heady scent of Hong Kong Island's biggest temple, creaking under the gaze of a dozen skyscrapers*

○ **Chan Shing Kee (p84)** *Browsing for genuine Chinese antiques*

○ **Sun Hing (p81)** *Eating old-school dim sum in up-and-coming Kennedy Town*

○ **Black Salt (p81)** *Dining at a great Sai Ying Pun neighbourhood joint*

Getting There & Around

🛳 The Hong Kong–Macau Ferry Terminal has regular ferry departures to Macau and some to Guǎngdōng in mainland China.

🚌 City buses heading to all parts of Hong Kong Island and Kowloon depart from the Macau Ferry Pier Bus Terminus.

🚊 The double-decker heritage tram runs along Des Voeux Rd Central and Des Voeux Rd West through Sheung Wan.

Neighbourhood Map on p76

Dried goods store, Sheung Wan wholesale district (p75)
SAIKO3P / SHUTTERSTOCK ©

Top Sight 📷
Man Mo Temple

One of Hong Kong's oldest temples, atmospheric Man Mo Temple is dedicated to the god of literature (Man), who's always holding a writing brush, and the god of war (Mo), who wields a sword.

◉ **MAP P76, F4**

文武廟

☏ 852 2540 0350

124-126 Hollywood Rd, Sheung Wan

admission free

🕗 8am-6pm

🚌 26

History

Built in 1847 during the Qing dynasty by wealthy Chinese merchants, it was, besides a place of worship, a court of arbitration for local disputes when trust was thin between the Chinese and the colonialists. Oaths taken at this Taoist temple (often accompanied by the ritual beheading of a rooster) were accepted by the colonial government.

The Temple Today

Outside the main entrance are four **gilt plaques** on poles that used to be carried around at processions. Two describe the gods being worshipped inside, one requests silence and a show of respect within the temple's grounds, and the last warns menstruating women to keep out of the main hall. Inside the temple (on the left as you go in) are two 19th-century sedan chairs with elaborate carvings, which used to carry statues of the two gods during festivals.

Lending the temple its beguiling and smoky air are rows of large earth-coloured spirals suspended from the roof, like strange fungi in an upside-down garden. These are incense coils burned as offerings by worshippers.

On the western side of the temple is **Lit Shing Kung** (the Saints' Palace), a place of worship for other Buddhist and Taoist deities. Another hall, **Kung Sor** (Public Meeting Place), used to serve as a court of justice to settle disputes among the Chinese community before the modern judicial system was introduced. A couplet at the entrance urges those entering to leave their selfish interests and prejudices outside. Fortune-tellers beckon from inside.

★ Top Tips

○ There are fortune-telling sticks (HK$100) to the right of the main altar at the back – slowly shake a stick out of the jar, then read the corresponding fortune in the (English) book.

○ As with all Chinese temples, don't step directly on the door's high threshold, but over it – the threshold is meant to keep bad spirits away.

✗ Take a Break

Sample French fusion dim sum at Man Mo Café (p80), just a few minutes' walk down Hollywood Rd in the thick of Cat Street Market.

Relax with a cuppa at Teakha (p83), on arty Tai Ping Shan St.

Walking Tour 🥾

Hong Kong's Wholesale District

Sheung Wan became a trading hub in the mid-19th century, when turmoil in China caused Chinese business owners to flee to Hong Kong. They set up businesses in Sheung Wan, trading in dried seafood, herbs and rice. As more migrants came, the area around Tai Ping Shan St became the heart of the Chinese community, with its own temples and funeral parlours.

Walk Facts

Start Sutherland St stop, Kennedy Town tram

End Sheung Wan MTR station, exit B

Length 1.5km; one hour

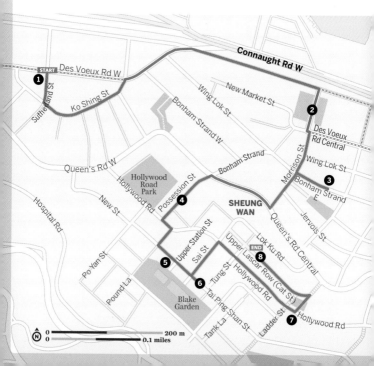

❶ Dried Seafood Street

Set off from the Sutherland St stop of the Kennedy Town tram. Have a look at (and a sniff of) Des Voeux Rd West's many dried sea-food shops piled with all manner of desiccated sea life. Walk south on Sutherland St to Ko Shing St to browse the medieval-looking goods on offer from the herbal-medicine traders.

❷ Western Market

At the end of Ko Shing St, re-enter Des Voeux Rd West and head northeast. Continue along Connaught Rd West, where you'll find the attractive colonial building that houses the **Western Market** (西港城; 323 Des Voeux Rd Central & New Market St; ⏰9am-7pm). Textile vendors driven off nearby streets in the 1990s now live on the first floor of this renovated Edwardian market building (1906).

❸ Lam Kie Yuen Tea Co

At the corner of Morrison St, walk south past Wing Lok St and onto Bonham Strand where you'll find **Lam Kie Yuen Tea Co** (林奇苑茶行; www.lkytea.com; Ground fl, 105-107 Bonham Strand E; ⏰9am-6pm Mon-Sat). It's been around since 1955 and is testament to just how much tea there is in China. From unfermented to fully fermented, and everything in between – the owner will offer you a tasting.

❹ Possession Street

Backtrack to climb up Possession St, where British marines planted the Union Jack flag in 1841 (look out for the plaque), then take a left into Hollywood Rd, before turning right to ascend Pound Lane to where it meets Tai Ping Shan St and a handful of temples.

❺ Kwun Yam Temple

Built in 1840, Sheung Wan's oldest **temple** (觀音廟; 34 Tai Ping Shan St; ⏰7.30am-5.30pm) honours Kwun Yam, the Goddess of Mercy. It's a quaint-looking structure, with a magnificent and intricate brass carving just above the doorway, and a yellow awning printed with Buddhist swastika symbols. Nearby is Pak Sing Ancestral Hall (p78).

❻ Tai Ping Shan Street

Once part of a plague-ridden Chinese tenement 'hood, trendy Tai Ping Shan St has become a breeding ground for upstart designers, small indie cafes and antiques shops that are being pushed further out of Central by soaring rents. Keep an eye out for street art in the surrounding alleys.

❼ Man Mo Temple

Turn north and descend to Hollywood Rd's antique shops where rare, mostly Chinese, treasures can be found. Continuing east brings you to Man Mo Temple (p72), one of the oldest and most significant temples in the territory.

❽ Cat Street Market

Take a short hop down Ladder St to Cat Street Market (p78), which is well stocked with inexpensive Chinese memorabilia. Sheung Wan MTR station is a little further downhill.

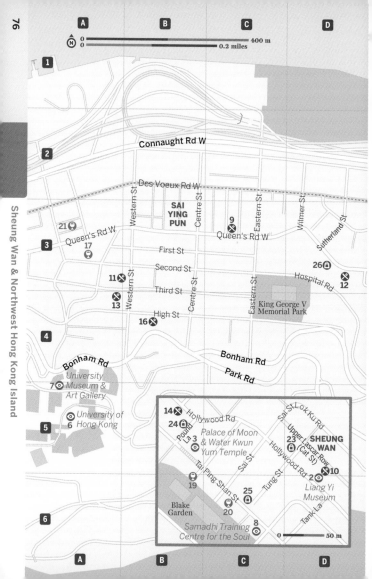

Sheung Wan & Northwest Hong Kong Island

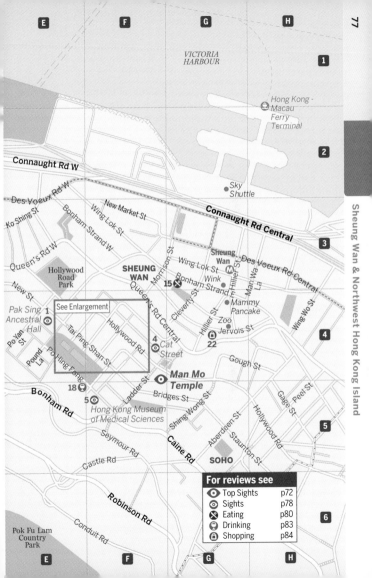

E **F** **G** **H**

1

VICTORIA HARBOUR

Hong Kong - Macau Ferry Terminal

2

Connaught Rd W

Des Voeux Rd W

New Market St

Connaught Rd Central

Sky Shuttle

3

Ko Shing St

Bonham Strand W

Wing Lok St

Sheung Wan

Wing Lok St

Des Voeux Rd Central

Queen's Rd W

Hollywood Road Park

SHEUNG WAN

Morrison St

Bonham Strand E

Man Wa La

New St

Queen's Rd Central

15 ✕

Wink

Hillier St

Mammy Pancake

Wing Wo St

Pak Sing Ancestral Hall

See Enlargement

Cleverly St

Zoo

Jervois St

22 🔒

4

Po Yan St

Tai Ping Shan St

Hollywood Rd

4 🔘 Cat Street

Gough St

Pound La

Po Hing Fong

18 🔒

Ladder St

Man Mo Temple

Peel St

Gage St

Hollywood Rd

5

Bonham Rd

5 🔒

Hong Kong Museum of Medical Sciences

Bridges St

Shing Wong St

Aberdeen St

Staunton St

Seymour Rd

Caine Rd

Castle Rd

SOHO

Robinson Rd

6

Pok Fu Lam Country Park

Conduit Rd

For reviews see
🔘	Top Sights	p72
🔘	Sights	p78
✕	Eating	p80
🍺	Drinking	p83
🔒	Shopping	p84

E **F** **G** **H**

Sights

Pak Sing
Ancestral Hall

TEMPLE

1 ◉ MAP P76, E4

In the 19th century many Chinese who left home in search of better horizons died overseas. As it was the wish of traditional Chinese to be buried in their home towns, this temple was built in 1856 to store corpses awaiting burial in China, and to serve as a public ancestral hall for those who could not afford the expense of bone repatriation. Families of the latter have erected 3000 memorial tablets for their ancestors in a room behind the altar. (廣福祠; Kwong Fuk Ancestral Hall; 42 Tai Ping Shan St, Sheung Wan; ⏱8am-5pm; 🚌26)

Liang Yi Museum

MUSEUM

2 ◉ MAP P76, D6

This private three-floor museum houses two exquisite collections: antique Chinese furniture from the Ming and Qing dynasties, and Chinese-inspired European vanities from the 19th and 20th century. The former is one of the world's best. The precious collection is displayed through rotating themed exhibitions that change every six months, paired with museum pieces called in from world-class galleries all over the globe. The museum itself is a stunning space; visits are by appointment only (book at least a day ahead) and by guided tour. (兩依博物館; 📞852

2806 8280; www.liangyimuseum.com; 181-199 Hollywood Rd, Soho; HK$200; ⏱by appointment 10am-6pm Tue-Sat; Ⓜ Central, exit D2)

Palace of Moon
& Water Kwun
Yum Temple

BUDDHIST TEMPLE

3 ◉ MAP P76, B5

Not to be confused with Kwun Yum Temple (p75) nearby, this dimly lit temple honours Kwun Yum of a Thousand Arms. Kwun Yum (aka Guanyin) is the Goddess of Compassion. According to legend, Buddha gave her a thousand arms so she could help everyone who needed it. For a small donation, you can give the small wooden windmill at the entrance a spin; it will presumably change your luck. (水月觀音堂; 7 Tai Ping Shan St, Sheung Wan; ⏱9am-6pm; 🚌26)

Cat Street

AREA

4 ◉ MAP P76, F4

Just north of (and parallel to) Hollywood Rd is Upper Lascar Row, aka 'Cat Street', a pedestrian-only lane lined with antique and curio shops and stalls selling Bruce Lee movie posters and old Hong Kong photos, cheap jewellery and newly minted ancient coins. It's a fun place to trawl through for souvenirs, but expect most artefacts to be mass-produced fakes. (摩囉街; Upper Lascar Row, Sheung Wan; ⏱10am-6pm; 🚌26)

Hong Kong Museum of Medical Sciences

MUSEUM

5 ◎ MAP P76, F5

Although this museum's focus is medical sciences, there are several interesting exhibits for tourists – in particular the section dedicated to the history of the Tai Ping Shan District in which the museum stands, now a hipster 'hood of little indie shops, bars and cafes, but once a vast slum area of tenement housing. It was here in 1894 that an outbreak of bubonic plague originated, turning Hong Kong into a quarantined port and making the British rethink health and medicine in the colony. (香港醫學博物館; 🕿852 2549 5123; www.hkmms.org.hk; 2 Caine Lane, Mid-Levels; adult/concession HK$20/10; ⏰10am-5pm Tue-Sat, 1-5pm Sun; 🚌3B)

University of Hong Kong

UNIVERSITY

6 ◎ MAP P76, A5

Established in 1911, HKU is the oldest university in Hong Kong. The Edwardian-style Main Building, with its pastel-pink edifice, colonnaded verandahs and red-brick core, dates to 1912 and is a declared monument. Several other early-20th-century buildings on the campus, including the domed Hung Hing Ying (1919), opposite the main entrance, and Tang Chi Ngong Buildings (1929), are also protected. (香港大學; 🕿852 2859 2111; www.hku.hk; Pok Fu Lam Rd, Pok Fu Lam; 🚌23, 40 from Admiralty)

Cat Street

University Museum & Art Gallery

MUSEUM

7 ◉ MAP P76, A5

The University of Hong Kong's Museum & Art Gallery houses collections of ceramics and bronzes spanning 5000 years, including exquisite blue-and-white Ming porcelain; early Qing dynasty furniture; and almost 1000 fascinating small Nestorian (Church of the East) crosses from the Yuan dynasty, the largest such collection in the world. It also hosts temporary exhibitions from around the world, covering everything from Italian Medici sculpture to photojournalism in Mongolia. (📞852 2241 5500; www.hku.hk/hkumag; Fung Ping Shan Bldg, 94 Bonham Rd, Pok Fu Lam; admission free; ⏰9.30am-6pm Mon-Sat, 1-6pm Sun; 🚍23, 40M)

Samadhi Training Centre for the Soul

MEDITATION

8 ◉ MAP P76, C6

Finding Hong Kong a bit full-on? Samadhi is here to help. At ground level there's a soothing meditation drop-in space that welcomes frazzled peace-seekers (tourists included), and above that there's a second space for weekly guided sessions, which often involve sound healing. The program is on its Facebook page; most events are free, but book ahead. (📞852 9311 2915; www.facebook.com/samadhicentre; 2-4 Tai Ping Shan St, Sheung Wan; ⏰11am-7pm Wed-Mon; 🚍26)

Eating

Kwun Kee Restaurant

CANTONESE $

9 ❌ MAP P76, C3

Hong Kong's top brass make pilgrimages to this local place for its claypot rice (HK$80 to HK$105, available only at dinner) – a meal-in-one in which rice and toppings such as chicken are cooked in claypots over charcoal stoves until the grains are infused with the juices of the meat and a layer of crackle is formed at the bottom. Enter from Kwai Heung St. (坤記煲仔小菜; 📞852 2803 7209; Wo Yick Mansion, 263 Queen's Rd W, Sai Ying Pun, Western District; meals from HK$80; ⏰11am-2.30pm & 6-11pm Mon-Sat, 6-11pm Sun; 🚍101)

Man Mo Café

DIM SUM $$

10 ❌ MAP P76, D5

At this welcoming place, chefs from culinary giants in Taiwan (Din Tai Fung) and France (Robuchon) team up to create high-end fusion dim sum. Portions are dainty but unique and utterly delicious. Rich foie gras explodes out of *xiao long bao* (soup dumplings), Nutella oozes from sesame-speckled balls, and truffle brie dumplings bewitch vegetarians. The chic interior reflects both its French influences and antique-y Cat St location. (📞852 2644 5644; www.manmodimsum.com; 40 Upper Lascar Row, Sheung Wan; meals HK$300-500;

🕑 noon-10.30pm Mon-Sat, to 5pm Sun; 🛜🍴; Ⓜ Central, exit D2)

Black Salt
ASIAN $$

11 ✖ MAP P76, A3

Black Salt is the friendly neighbourhood restaurant we'd all like to have around the corner. It's tiny inside (so book ahead), and tables spill out onto a small laneway terrace. Dishes are a delicious, accomplished mash-up of South Asian cuisines, including fancy Kathmandu *momo* dumplings, Sri Lankan *kothu roti* and Indian *mattar paneer* with melt-in-the-mouth homemade curds. Service is split into two sittings. (📞852 3702 1237, reservations by Whatsapp 852 5173 3058; www.blacksalt.com.hk; Ground fl, 14 Fuk Sau Lane, Sai Ying Pun; meals from HK$300; 🕑5.30-11pm Tue-Sat, to

10pm Sun, noon-3pm Sat & Sun; 🛜🍴; Ⓜ Sai Ying Pun, exit B2)

Okra
JAPANESE $$

12 ✖ MAP P76, D3

This relaxed *izakaya* (informal Japanese pub) in Sai Ying Pun is as much about sake sampling as it is the food, but the enthusiastic staff nail both. The team work closely with trusted producers to bring the best natural and unpasteurised sakes to Hong Kong, then match them with creative dishes such as crispy brussels sprouts with homemade XO sauce and smoked *yuzu* jam ribs. (📞852 2806 1038; www.okra.kitchen; Ground fl, 110 Queen's Rd W, Sai Ying Pun; meals from HK$400; 🕑6-11.30pm Mon-Sat; 🛜; Ⓜ Sai Ying Pun, exit A1)

Hong Kong Island's Wild West 🢂

Ride the MTR's Island line to its most westerly point (or take the double-decker tram) and you'll emerge in Kennedy Town, a quiet neighbourhood at the foot of Mt Davis that feels a lot further away from Central's skyscrapers than it actually is. This is where Hong Kong life meets the edge of Victoria Harbour and fishermen still plunge their rods into the sea straight off the Praya.

Hong Kong's foodies know Kennedy Town for one thing above all: dim sum at **Sun Hing** (新興食家; 📞852 2816 0616; Ground fl, 8C Smithfield Rd, Kennedy Town, Western District; meals HK$50; 🕑3am-4pm; 🚌101). Arrive early or extremely late (as in, 5am) to see taxi drivers and city workers get their fix at this working-class joint. Finish your explorations with craft beers at Aussie microbrewery **Little Creatures** (📞852 2833 5611; www.littlecreatures.hk; Ground fl, 5A New Praya, Kennedy Town; 🕑9am-11.30pm Mon-Fri, 8am-11pm Sat & Sun; 🛜); the surest sign that gentrification is coming this way.

Hong Kong's Egg Waffle

Hong Kong is a city of foodie fad-followers and one of its original inventions is the bulbous egg puff/waffle, sometimes filled with treats like red bean or peanut butter. Many locals will argue that Michelin-recommended **Mammy Pancake** (媽咪雞蛋仔; Map p76, G4; 32 Bonham Strand E, Sheung Wan; waffles from HK$16; ⏰noon-9pm) whips up the fluffiest and best. Place your order at the counter and wait for your paper bag. Add an iced tea for extra street cred.

Potato Head   INDONESIAN $$

13 ✕ MAP P76, A4

The Hong Kong outpost of Potato Head, which started as a hipster beach club in Bali with killer cocktails, isn't so much a restaurant as a multiconcept events space with food and decks. It consists of an excellent Indonesian restaurant, Kaum, where you eat small plates off a long wooden table; a fun cocktail lounge; and a hidden Music Room at the back. (☎852 2858 6066; www.ptthead. com; Ground fl, 100 Third St, Sai Ying Pun; meals HK$150-400; ⏰restaurant noon-11pm Mon-Fri, from 11am Sat & Sun; ❄🛜; Ⓜ Sai Ying Pun, exit B2)

Chachawan   THAI $$

14 ✕ MAP P76, B5

Specialising in the spicy cuisine of northeastern Thailand's Isaan region, this hip little spot is always jam-packed and plenty noisy. No curries or pad thai here, just bright, herb-infused, chilli-packed salads and grilled fish and meat (vegetarian options too). Wash it all down with cocktails incorporating Thai flavours such as sweet tea and lychee. No reservations – expect a wait in the evening. (☎852 2549 0020; www.chachawan.hk; Ground fl, 206 Hollywood Rd, Sheung Wan; meals HK$200-450; ⏰noon-3pm & 6.30-11pm, happy hour 5-7pm; 🛜🚭; Ⓜ Sheung Wan, exit A2)

Tim's Kitchen   CANTONESE $$

15 ✕ MAP P76, G3

This two-floor formal restaurant is considered one of Hong Kong's best – as evidenced by the Michelin honour and the praises lavished by local gourmets. It serves extraordinarily delicate and subtle Cantonese fare, and at lunchtimes a reasonably priced dim sum menu too. Signature items such as the crab claw poached with wintermelon and crystal king prawn require pre-ordering a day ahead. Reservations essential. (桃花源; ☎852 2543 5919; www.timskitchen.com.hk; 84-90 Bonham Strand, Sheung Wan; lunch HK$130-500, dinner HK$300-1000; ⏰11am-3pm & 6-11pm; 🚽; Ⓜ Sheung Wan, exit A2)

Cross Cafe CAFE $

16 🗶 MAP P76, B4

Taking its cue from the traditional Hong Kong *cha chaan tang* (teahouse), this cafe with minimalist white seating and red neon signs offers a contemporary twist on the much-loved original. Dishes such as oatmeal in Trappist mango papaya milk, or fluffy pineapple bun with truffled scrambled egg, make for a satisfying breakfast. There's no English sign; look for the neon Chinese characters. (十字冰室; ☑852 2887 1315; www.facebook.com/crosscafehk; Shop 12, Ground fl, Hang Sing Mansion, 48-78 High St, Sai Ying Pun, Western District; breakfast/meals from HK$30/40; ⏰7.30am-8.30pm Mon-Sun; Ⓜ Sai Ying Pun, exit B2, minibus 12)

Drinking

Ping Pong Gintoneria BAR

17 🍸 MAP P76, A3

Behind a closed red door, stairs lead down into a cavernous former ping-pong hall, now one of Hong Kong's coolest bars. The drink here is gin – the neon-illuminated bar stocks more than 50 types from across the globe, served in a variety of cocktails both classic and creative (G&Ts from HK$110). The crowd is artsy, and the decor is even artsier. (☑852 9835 5061; www.pingpong129.com; 135 Second St, Sai Ying Pun; ⏰4.30pm-midnight Sun-Thu, to 1am Fri & Sat; 🛜; Ⓜ Sai Ying Pun, exit B2)

Cupping Room COFFEE

18 🚇 MAP P76, E5

The moreish, heady scent of freshly roasting coffee is amplified in this speciality coffee shop, thanks to the roasting room directly behind the counter. Cupping Room has several branches in Hong Kong but this is where the magic happens. The cafe is atypically roomy, and a lovely place to pause after browsing the nearby Tai Ping Shan area. It's also popular for brunch. (☑852 3705 0208; www.cuppingroom.hk; Shop 8, Silver Jubilee Mansion, Po Hing Fong, Sheung Wan; ⏰9am-5pm Mon-Fri, to 6pm Sat & Sun; 🛜; 🚌26)

Craftissimo CRAFT BEER

19 🚇 MAP P76, B6

Look for the kegs turned into squat bar stools down an alley off Tai Ping Shan St and you'll find this laid-back bottle shop and craft-beer bar. There's no seating inside, just six rotating draught taps and a wall crammed with local and international craft beers that you can buy to take away or drink on the charming, rough-and-ready patio. (☑852 6274 3130; www.craftissimo.hk; Shop D, Ground fl, 22-24 Tai Ping Shan St, Sheung Wan; ⏰1-10pm Sun-Thu, to 11pm Fri & Sat; 🚌26)

Teakha TEAHOUSE

20 🚇 MAP P76, C6

Fancy organic tea concoctions are best enjoyed with the homemade drop scones in this modern interpretation of a Chinese teahouse,

Sheung Wan's LGBT Scene

Hong Kong's LGBT scene is surprisingly small for the city's size and worldliness, but a community does exist and it is friendly, inclusive and growing in confidence. In recent years a pocket of bars and clubs has put down roots in Sheung Wan and in 2018 three of them joined together to promote the area as a 'Gaybarhood'. Its epicentre is around Jervois St and Bonham Strand and so far the 'hood includes **Zoo** (Map p76, G4; ☑ 852 3583 1200; www.facebook.com/Zoo BarHK; Ground fl, 33 Jervois St, Sheung Wan; ◷ 7pm-4.30am; 🛜; Ⓜ Sheung Wan, exit A2), **Wink** (Map p76, G3; ☑ 852 3568 1402; www.facebook.com/winkhongkong; Ground fl, 79 Bonham Strand, Sheung Wan; ◷ 5.30pm-3am Mon-Fri, from 8pm Sat & Sun, happy hour 5-9pm Mon-Fri; 🛜) and **FLM** (☑ 852 2799 2883; www.flmhk.net; 62 Jervois St, Sheung Wan), which are all within easy crawling distance. Keep an eye on the website (www.gaybarhood.net) and Facebook page for deals, events and local LGBT news.

just off the main street in the impossibly hip Tai Ping Shan St area. The cute teaware makes a good souvenir. (茶家; ☑ 852 2858 9185; www.teakha.com; Shop B, 18 Tai Ping Shan St, Sheung Wan; ◷ 9am-6pm Mon & Wed-Fri, 8.30am-7pm Sat & Sun; 🛜; 🚌 26)

Junels Resto Bar

BAR

21 🚇 MAP P76, A3

A local favourite among Western District residents, Junels Resto Bar is a Philippine restaurant with a difference (basically, you won't come here for the food). After dark, it turns into a free-for-all karaoke joint, with groups of friends screeching through a generous selection of hits. The San Miguels are cheap and it's decorated like a Christmas tree all year round.

(☑ 852 5182 8725; Ground fl, 11 Lai On Lane, Water St, Sai Ying Pun; ◷ noon-late; Ⓜ Sai Ying Pun, exit B3)

Shopping

Chan Shing Kee

ANTIQUES

22 🔒 MAP P76, G4

This shop with a three-storey, museum-like showroom is run by Daniel Chan, the third generation of a family that's been in the business for 70 years. Chan Shing Kee is known to collectors and museums worldwide for its fine classical Chinese furniture (16th to 18th century). Scholars' objects, such as ancient screens and wooden boxes, are also available. (陳勝記; ☑ 852 2543 1245; www.chanshingkee.com; 228-230 Queen's Rd Central, Sheung Wan; ◷ 9am-6pm Mon-Sat; 🚌 101, 104)

Capital Gallery

ANTIQUES

23 🔒 MAP P76, D5

Located on a slope between Upper Lascar Row and Hollywood Rd, this tiny, friendly shop specialises in ceramics and is crammed with sculptures and other curios dating from 4000 to 5000 years ago. Silk Road pieces, such as minority textiles from northwest China, are also a highlight. (長安美術; ☏852 2542 2271; 27E Tung St, Sheung Wan; ⏰10am-6pm Mon-Sat, by appointment Sun; 🚃26, Ⓜ Central, exit D2)

Niin

JEWELLERY

24 🔒 MAP P76, B5

Ever wondered what happens to all the abalone shells thrown out by Hong Kong's restaurants? Some of them end up here, reimagined as beautiful pendants, rings, bracelets and handbags. Australian–Hong Kong designer Jeanine Hsu uses shells, reclaimed wood, brass and natural gemstones in her unusual but very wearable creations. Prices start at about HK$1200. (☏852 2878 8811; www.niinstyle. com; 200 Hollywood Rd, Sheung Wan; ⏰10am-7pm Mon-Wed & Fri, 11am-8pm Thu, 11am-6pm Sat)

Only Alice

FASHION & ACCESSORIES

25 🔒 MAP P76, C6

In an area spoilt for choice with independent fashion, this contemporary Hong Kong brand stands out with its wearable clothing and reasonable prices. Playful tees, flattering utility wear and feminine florals are all present in this small Tai Ping Shan store, along with accessories like headbands and off-the-wall stockings. Expect to pay well under HK$1000 for most pieces. (☏852 3464 0772; www. theonlyalice.com; Ground fl, 55 Tung St, Sheung Wan; ⏰9.30am-6.30pm Tue-Fri, 10am-7pm Sat & Sun; 🚃26)

Queen's Road West Incense Shops

ARTS & CRAFTS

26 🔒 MAP P76, D3

At 136–150 Queen's Rd West, there are shops selling incense and paper offerings for the dead. The latter are burned to propitiate departed souls and the choice of combustibles is mind-blowing – dim sum, iPads, Rolexes, Viagra tablets and even solar-powered water heaters. You may buy them as souvenirs, but keeping rather than burning them is supposed to bring bad luck. (Queen's Rd W, Sheung Wan; ⏰8am-7pm; 🚃26)

Explore ◈
Wan Chai, Admiralty & Causeway Bay

Wan Chai is Hong Kong distilled: a towering, tireless show-case of the old and new. To its west, Admiralty is home to government headquarters, quality shopping and dining, and mind-blowing hill and sea views. In the shopping mecca of Causeway Bay, traffic, malls and restaurants jockey with a cemetery and the Happy Valley Racecourse.

The Short List

○ **Blue House Cluster (p94)** *Uncovering heritage architecture around Queen's Rd East, alongside hipster bars, temples, markets and bazaars*

○ **Happy Valley Racecourse (p118)** *Feeling your adrenaline soar at an urban racecourse on a Wednesday night, beer in hand*

○ **Fashion Walk (p105)** *Trawling through the streets and malls for designer fashion among the hordes of teenyboppers in Causeway Bay*

○ **Flagstaff House Museum of Tea Ware (p95)** *Experiencing culture, history and gastronomy at this heritage museum in Hong Kong Park*

Getting There & Around

🚋 Hennessy Rd is a good place to catch trams to Central and Causeway Bay. Happy Valley trams use Percival St.

🚌 5, 5B and 26 link Central and Sheung Wan with Admiralty, Causeway Bay and Happy Valley.

Ⓜ The Island Line and South Island Line intersect at Admiralty station; the Tseung Kwan O Line to Kowloon runs through North Point.

⚓ Wan Chai ferry pier connects with Tsim Sha Tsui, Kowloon. North Point pier goes to Hung Hom.

Neighbourhood Map on p92

Happy Valley Racecourse (p105) GAVIN HELLIER / ROBERTHARDING / GETTY IMAGES ©

Top Sight 📷
Hong Kong Park

Designed to look anything but natural, the hillside oasis of Hong Kong Park emphasises artificial creations such as its fountain plaza, cascading waterfall, playground and aviary, connected by terraced landscaping and tree-lined pathways. Yet the 8-hectare park is beautiful and, with a wall of skyscrapers on one side and mountains on the other, makes for dramatic photographs.

◉ MAP P92, A3

香港公園

www.lcsd.gov.hk/en/
parks/hkp/index.html

19 Cotton Tree Dr,
Admiralty

🕙 park 6am-11pm

Ⓜ Admiralty, exit C1

Edward Youde Aviary & Forsgate Conservatory

The standout feature of Hong Kong Park is the **Edward Youde Aviary** (尤德觀鳥園; admission free; ⏱9am-5pm). Home to some 80 bird species, it's something akin to a rainforest planted in the middle of the city. Visitors walk along a wooden gantry several metres above the ground and at eye level with tree branches. The aviary is named after a former Hong Kong governor (1982–86).

Flagstaff House Museum of Tea Ware

At the park's northernmost tip is the elegant colonial residence Flagstaff House (p95). Built in 1846 for a British Major-General, it now houses a museum of antique Chinese teaware: bowls, brewing trays, sniffing cups and teapots made of porcelain or purple clay from Yíxìng. The adjacent Lock Cha Tea Shop (p97) is a great place to recharge over a pot of fine tea and vegetarian dim sum.

KS Lo Gallery

The exquisite **KS Lo Gallery** (羅桂祥茶藝館; ☎852 2869 0690; 10 Cotton Tree Dr, Admiralty; admission free; ⏱10am-6pm Wed-Mon) above Lock Cha Tea Shop (p97) contains rare Chinese ceramics from renowned kilns in ancient China, as well as stone seals owned by the eponymous collector.

Hong Kong Visual Arts Centre

On the eastern edge of the park, the **Hong Kong Visual Arts Centre** (香港視覺藝術中心; ☎852 2521 3008; 7A Kennedy Rd, Admiralty; admission free; ⏱10am-6pm Wed-Mon; ▣3B, 12, 12A), housed in part of the former Victoria Barracks, stages occasional exhibitions of multimedia works by local and Asian artists. Much of the barracks was demolished to create Hong Kong Park in the late 1980s.

★ Top Tips

○ Lock Cha Tea Shop has popular Chinese music performances on Saturday (7pm to 8.30pm) and Sunday (4.30pm to 6.30pm).

○ The aviary is stroller accessible; Hong Kong Park also has an outdoor kids' play area.

○ Kids will love the ponds, pools and streams filled with cute turtles and darting koi carp.

○ Combine your trip with a saunter around the Asia Society Hong Kong Centre (p94).

✕ Take a Break

Recharge over tea and vegetarian dim sum at antique-styled Lock Cha Tea Shop (p97).

Head to **Petit Cafe** (☎852 2918 9293; Shop 407, Pacific Pl, 88 Queensway, Admiralty; ⏱7.30am-9.30pm, from 8.30am Sun; ▣Admiralty, exit F) above Pacific Place and join the worker bees for crisp panini, espresso and wines by the glass.

Walking Tour 🚶

Old Wan Chai's Forgotten Streets

Wan Chai's coastline used to run near the tram tracks on Johnston Rd before zealous land reclamation pushed the shoreline to the north. The area around Queen's Rd East and Johnston Rd was a fishing village with shrines and temples overlooking the sea. After the British came, shipyards were built along the bay and Europeans made their homes in the hills south of Queen's Rd East.

Walk Facts

Start Pak Tai Temple
End Star St
Length 1.2km; two hours

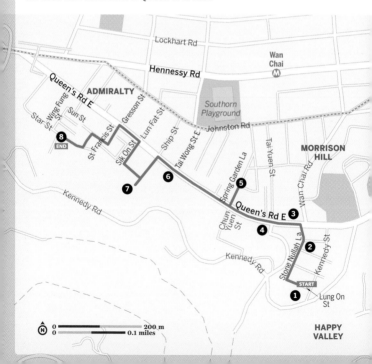

❶ Pak Tai Temple

A short stroll from the main bus routes and Wan Chai metro (exit A3), you'll start to get a feel for the neighbourhood as it was in the 19th century at Pak Tai Temple (p94), a stunning temple built 150 years ago by local residents.

❷ Blue House

Further down the slope, the Blue House (p96), one of Hong Kong's last surviving wooden tenement buildings, will show you what life was like in Wan Chai in the last century via its fascinating House of Stories.

❸ The Original Wan Chai Market

The Streamline Moderne exterior of the original Wan Chai Market (corner Queen's Rd East and Wan Chai Rd) is all that remains of the place, which now fronts a shopping centre. Once the hub of the neighbourhood, the market was used as a mortuary by Japanese forces in WWII (the new, air-conditioned market is at number 258).

❹ Old Wan Chai Post Office

Pocket-sized **Old Wan Chai Post Office** (舊灣仔郵政局; 221 Queen's Rd E; ⏱10am-5pm Mon-Wed) operated from 1915 to 1992 and is Hong Kong's oldest post office. These days it's a resource centre for the Environmental Protection Department. Pop inside and you'll see they've retained the worn wooden counter, post-office boxes and a stamp vending machine.

❺ Spring Garden Lane

Take a quick look at Spring Garden Lane, one of the first areas developed by the British, and imagine what it was like when prostitutes solicited here in the 1900s.

❻ Hung Shing Temple

Head along Queen's Rd East to peep inside the mysterious **Hung Shing Temple** (洪聖古廟; 129-131 Queen's Rd E; ⏱8.30am-5.30pm), once a seaside shrine in the days when the sea came right up to the temple doors. It was erected around 1850 in honour of a deified Tang dynasty official known for his virtue (important) and ability to make predictions of value to traders (ultra-important).

❼ Ghost House

Just west of the temple, turn up the hill along Ship St and stand before the now derelict Ghost House at 55 Nam Koo Tce. Its history is a wretched one: it was used by Japanese soldiers as a brothel housing 'comfort women' in WWII.

❽ Star Street

The Star St neighbourhood is a quietly hip corner of town with street names (Star, Sun, Moon) that indicate this was the site of Hong Kong's first power plant. On 31 Wing Fung St is a six-storey balconied building in art deco style. Admiralty MTR can be reached by an escalator and underground travelator entered at the bottom of Wing Fung St.

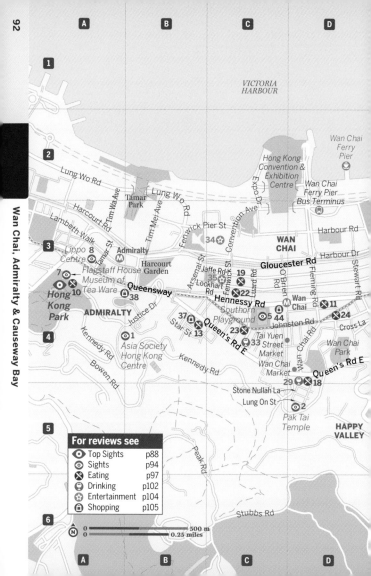

Wan Chai, Admiralty & Causeway Bay

VICTORIA HARBOUR

Wan Chai Ferry Pier

Lung Wo Rd

Tamar Park

Harcourt Rd

Lambeth Walk

Lippo Centre 8 Admiralty

7 Flagstaff House Museum of Tea Ware

Hong Kong Park

10

38

ADMIRALTY

Queensway

Justice Dr

1 Asia Society Hong Kong Centre

Kennedy Rd

Bowen Rd

Lung Wo Rd

Harcourt Garden

Star St

37 13

Kennedy Rd

Hong Kong Convention & Exhibition Centre

Wan Chai Ferry Pier Bus Terminus

WAN CHAI

Harbour Rd

Gloucester Rd

Harbour Dr

34

Jaffe Rd 19

35 Lockhart Rd

22

Hennessy Rd

Southorn Playground

5 44

Wan Chai

11

24

Cross La

Johnston Rd

23

Queen's Rd E

33

Tai Yuen Street Market

Wan Chai Market

Wan Chai Park

29 18

Queen's Rd E

Stone Nullah La

Lung On St

2

Pak Tai Temple

HAPPY VALLEY

Peak Rd

Stubbs Rd

For reviews see

⊙	Top Sights	p88
⊙	Sights	p94
✕	Eating	p97
⬤	Drinking	p102
★	Entertainment	p104
🔒	Shopping	p105

N 0 ———— 500 m
   0 ———— 0.25 miles

Island Eastern Corridor

Watson Rd

4
21
31
1

King's Rd

Ring Fat St

20
32
TIN HAU
2

Cross-Harbour Tunnel

Causeway Bay Typhoon Shelter

Causeway Bay

Kellett Island

Tsing Fung St

Electric Rd

Houston St

Victoria Park
9

14

Tin Hau
M
3
Tin Hau Temple

CAUSEWAY BAY

Gloucester Rd
25
12
36
28
Paterson St
Lockhart Rd

Gloucester Rd

Causeway Rd

Moreton Tce

3

27

Marsh Rd

26
16
Percival St
Jaffe Rd

Canal Rd

Jaffe Rd
Lockhart Rd
Hennessy Rd
15

Causeway Bay
M
39
Lee Kai Chiu
43
Russell St
40
Matheson St
Yun Ping Rd
Lee Garden Rd

41
Yee Wo St

Leighton Rd

Leighton Rd

Tung Lo Wan Rd
Wun Sha St

42
Tai Hang Rd

Wan Chai Rd
30
Yat Sin St
Yiu Wa St
Leighton Rd

CAROLINE HILL

Eastern Hospital Rd

Kai Hang Rd

TAI HANG
4

MORRISON HILL

Sports Rd

LEIGHTON HILL

Wong Nai Chung Rd

Link Rd

Caroline Hill Rd

Hong Kong Stadium

6
Hong Kong Cemetery

Happy Valley Racecourse

Ventris Rd

Broadwood Rd

Tai Hang Rd

5

Stubbs Rd

Wong Nai Chung Rd

Blue Pool Rd

Yuk Sau St
17
Sing Woo Rd

6

Aberdeen Tunnel

Sights

Asia Society Hong Kong Centre

CULTURAL CENTRE

1 ◉ MAP P92, B4

Hong Kong's Asia Society moved to these fabulous new digs in 2012, enclosing an art gallery, theatre, **restaurant** (☎852 2537 9888; www. ammo.com.hk; mains around HK$250; ◷noon-11pm Sun-Thu, to midnight Fri & Sat) and gift shop all open to the public. The hillside complex is a lovely place to wander, incorporating heritage buildings and former ammunition stores artfully linked by raised walkways and rooftop gardens. Architects Tod Williams and Billie Tsien opted for a low-rise design that deferred to history and the natural lie of the land, in contrast to the skyscrapers nearby. (亞洲協會香港中心; Hong Kong Jockey Club Former Explosives Magazine; ☎852 2103 9511; www.asiasociety. org/hong-kong; 9 Justice Dr, Admiralty; admission free; ◷gallery 11am-5pm Tue-Sun, to 7pm last Thu of month; Ⓜ Admiralty, exit F)

Pak Tai Temple

TAOIST TEMPLE

2 ◉ MAP P92, D5

A short stroll up Stone Nullah Lane takes you to a majestic Taoist temple built in 1863 to honour a god of the sea, Pak Tai. The temple, the largest on Hong Kong Island, is adorned with ceramic roof-ridge ornaments made in the Guǎngdōng pottery centre of Shíwān that depict scenes from Cantonese opera. The main hall of the temple has a shadowy, 3m-tall copper likeness of Pak Tai cast during the Ming dynasty. (北帝廟; 2 Lung On St, Wan Chai; ◷8am-5pm; Ⓜ Wan Chai, exit A3)

Tin Hau Temple

TEMPLE

3 ◉ MAP P92, H3

Hong Kong Island's most famous Tin Hau (Goddess of the Sea) temple has lent its name to an entire neighbourhood, a metro station and a street. It has been a place of worship for 370 years and, despite renovations, imparts an air of antiquity, particularly in the intricate stone carvings near the entrance and the ceramic figurines from Shíwān decorating the roof. The main altar contains an effigy of the goddess with a blackened face. (天后廟; 10 Tin Hau Temple Rd, Causeway Bay; ◷7am-5pm; Ⓜ Tin Hau, exit B)

Chun Yeung Street Market

MARKET

4 ◉ MAP P92, H1

Hop on a tram bound for North Point, and past Fortress Hill you'll turn into a narrow street teeming with market stalls and old tenement buildings. This is the famous Chun Yeung Street Market, and at 5pm it's so busy the tram has to squeeze between traders and cart-pullers. Many stores here sell foodstuffs from Fújiàn that you can't find elsewhere in Hong Kong. North Point has a huge Fújiànese community and you'll hear their dialect spoken on Chun Yeung St. (春秧街街市; Chun

Yeung St, North Point; ⏱8am-6pm;
Ⓜ North Point, exit A4)

Southorn Playground   PARK

5 ◉ MAP P92, C4

This unspectacular-looking sports
ground is in fact the social hub of
old Wan Chai, offering a cross-
section of life in the 'hood at any
time of the day. Seniors come to
play chess, students and amateur
athletes to shoot hoops and kick
ball. There are hip-hop dance-
offs, homemakers shaking a leg,
outreach social workers, cruisers
looking for a booty call, and a daily
trickle of lunchers from the banks
and construction sites. (修頓球
場; Hennessy Rd, Wan Chai; ⏱6am-
11.30pm; Ⓜ Wan Chai, exit B2)

Hong Kong Cemetery   CEMETERY

6 ◉ MAP P92, E5

Crowded and cosmopolitan, dead
Hong Kong is no different from the
breathing city. Tombstones jostle
for space at this Christian cemetery
(c 1845) located alongside the Jewish, Hindu, Parsee and Muslim cem-
eteries, and St Michael's Catholic
Cemetery. Burial plots date from
the mid-1800s and include colonialists, tycoons and silver-screen
divas. (香港墳場; Wong Nai Chung Rd,
Happy Valley; admission free; ⏱7am-
6pm or 7pm; 🚋Happy Valley)

Flagstaff House
Museum of Tea Ware   MUSEUM

7 ◉ MAP P92, A3

Built in 1846 as the home of the
commander of the British forces,

Tin Hau Temple

KEN WELSH / GETTY IMAGES ©

Blue House Cluster

A rare heritage protection success story, the 1920s **Blue House** (藍屋; www.vivabluehouse.hk; 72-74A Stone Nullah Lane, Wan Chai; ⓂWan Chai, exit D) is one of Hong Kong's last surviving wooden tenement buildings. The graceful, four-storey structure, featuring cast-iron balconies reminiscent of New Orleans, and its adjoining neighbours the Yellow House and Orange House, were taken over by a local community trust (thank heavens – it almost became a spa in the 2000s), painstakingly restored and are now partially open to the public. Several apartments still house descendants of the original residents.

Two eateries, a thrift store, community library and an organic veg shop in the cluster are being run as social enterprises, with all profits returning to the Blue House. Free guided tours in English (11am Saturdays) take you into a residential unit preserved as it was in the mid-20th century – you'll be astonished at how many families shared the same room. The **House of Stories**, a museum and exhibition space on the ground floor (10am to 6pm, closed Wednesday), is a rich source of info on yesteryear Hong Kong.

The Blue House was built atop a temple to the god of Chinese medicine, which was preserved within the new tenement. You can see the temple facade at the corner of King Sing St and Stone Nullah Lane.

Flagstaff House is the oldest colonial building in Hong Kong still standing in its original spot. Its colonnaded verandahs exude a Greek Revival elegance, complemented by the grace of the teaware from the 11th to the 20th centuries: bowls, brewing trays, sniffing cups (used particularly for enjoying the fragrance of the finest oolong from Taiwan) and teapots made of porcelain or purple clay from Yíxing. (旗桿屋茶具文物館; ☎852 2869 0690; 10 Cotton Tree Dr, Admiralty; admission free; ⏰10am-6pm Wed-Mon; ⓂAdmiralty, exit C1)

Lippo Centre

ARCHITECTURE

8 ◎ MAP P92, A3

Though the HSBC (Hongkong & Shanghai Bank) Building (p44) and the Hong Kong International Airport, both by English architect Norman Foster, may be Hong Kong's best-known examples of modern architecture, the city also features quite a number of fine modern buildings designed by old masters. The Lippo Centre, which evokes koalas hugging a tree, is a pair of office towers designed in the 1980s by American architect Paul Rudolph, who also built Rudolph Hall at the Yale School of

Architecture. (力寶中心; 89 Queensway, Admiralty; M Admiralty, exit B)

Victoria Park PARK

9 ⊚ MAP P92, G2

Built on land reclaimed from the **Causeway Bay Typhoon Shelter** (銅鑼灣避風塘), Victoria Park is the biggest patch of public greenery on Hong Kong Island. The best time to go is on a weekday morning, when it becomes a forest of people practising the slow-motion choreography of taichi. The park becomes a flower market just before the Lunar New Year and a lantern museum during the **Mid-Autumn Festival**. The swimming pool (previously outdoor), built in 1957, is Hong Kong's oldest. (維多利亞公園; www.lcsd.gov.hk/en/ls_park.php; Causeway Rd, Causeway Bay; admission free; ⏰ park 24hr; 👶; M Tin Hau, exit B)

Eating

Lock Cha Tea Shop VEGETARIAN, CHINESE $

10 ✖ MAP P92, A3

Set in the lush environs of Hong Kong Park, Lock Cha serves fragrant Chinese teas and vegetarian dim sum in an antique-styled environment designed to resemble a scholar's quarters. There are traditional music performances on Saturday (7pm to 8.30pm) and Sunday (4.30pm to 6.30pm). Do call to reserve a seat. (樂茶軒; ☎ 852 2801 7177; www.lockcha.com; Ground fl, KS Lo Gallery, 10 Cotton Tree

Dr, Hong Kong Park, Admiralty; dim sum HK$28-35, tea from HK$38; ⏰ 10am-8pm, to 9pm weekends, closed 2nd Tue of month; 🍴; M Admiralty, exit C1)

Kam's Roast Goose CANTONESE $

11 ✖ MAP P92, D4

Expect to queue for half an hour or more to worship at the oily altar of perfectly roasted goose. One of two spin-offs from Central's famed Yung Kee Restaurant (p62), Michelin-starred Kam's still upholds the same strict standards in sourcing and roasting. The best cut is the upper thigh (succulent but less fatty), which can be had with steamed rice or seasoned noodles. (甘牌燒鵝; ☎ 852 2520 1110; www.krg.com.hk; 226 Hennessy Rd, Wan Chai; meals HK$80-200; ⏰ 11.30am-9pm; M Wan Chai, exit A2)

Cafe Match Box HONG KONG $

12 ✖ MAP P92, F3

Whimsical Match Box is a hip shrine to the *bing sutt* of the 1950s (literally 'ice room'), the western-style cafe predecessor of the *cha chaan tang* (teahouse). Mandopop paraphernalia, an antique coke fridge and retro public bus booths set the scene for red-bean drinks, fluffy egg sandwiches, macaroni, oatmeal and toast. Lots of toast. The alleyway location adds to the atmosphere. (喜喜冰室; ☎ 852 2868 0363; www.cafematchbox.com.hk; 57 Paterson St, Causeway Bay; breakfast sets from HK$36; ⏰ 8am-11pm; M Causeway Bay, exit D1)

Wagyu beef noodles at Samsen

Honbo

BURGERS $

13 MAP P92, B4

The juicy *honbo* here (Cantonese for hamburger) are dainty, delicious and local, employing New Territories beef and veggies, and buns baked down the road. Like the mini dining room, the Cantonese chef-owner keeps the menu trim (beef and cheese, battered soft-shell crab or seared scallops), accompanied by excellent fries and a couple of Hong Kong craft beers on tap. (☎852 2567 8970; https://honbo.hk; 6-7 Sun St, Wan Chai; burgers from HK$88; ⏱noon-4pm & 5-10pm; Ⓜ Admiralty, exit F)

Sister Wah

NOODLES $

14 MAP P92, H2

Locals and tourists pack out this steamy corner eatery to slurp flat rice noodles topped with wobbly beef brisket or tendon in a clear soup broth. Old-timers like to chase theirs with a bowl of cooked white radish. (華姐清湯腩; ☎852 2807 0181; 13 Electric Rd, Tin Hau; noodles HK$48; ⏱11am-10.45pm; Ⓜ Tin Hau, exit A2)

DimDimSum

DIM SUM $

15 MAP P92, E3

There are few reliably good restaurants around town that continue to serve dim sum late into the evening (it's typically eaten for brunch). Then there's DimDimSum. The

Cantonese chain, which has several branches across Hong Kong, has all the classics: turnip cake, fluffy *char siu bao* (barbecue pork buns), pork and shrimp dumplings and crispy rice rolls, which are served to steaming-hot perfection. (📞852 3568 2770; www.dimdimsum.hk; 7 Tin Lok Lane, Wan Chai; dim sum HK$18-40; ⏱10am-11.30pm; Ⓜ Causeway Bay, exit A)

Atum Desserant
DESSERTS $

16 MAP P92, F3

Hop on to a stool at this Scandi-styled dessert bar and watch gallery-worthy creations materialise with some help from liquid nitrogen and the owner's years as a pastry chef at the Mandarin Oriental. Improvisation (HK$348 for two) is confectionary, fruits and ice cream 'painted' on a slab in front of you like a Jackson Pollock crossbred with a Monet. (📞852 2377 2400, 852 2956 1411; www.atumhk.com; 16th fl, The L Square,

459-461 Lockhart Rd, Causeway Bay; desserts from HK$138; ⏱1-11.30pm; 🍴; Ⓜ Causeway Bay, exit C)

Cheong Kee
HONG KONG $

17 MAP P92, G6

This scrappy little *dai pai dong* (大牌檔; food stall) above a wet market is one of Hong Kong's most venerable *cha chaan tangs*, beloved for its ultrathick toast drenched in condensed milk and peanut butter. Milk tea is silky-sweet, while local comfort foods such as pork-chop noodles and *char siu* with egg are well above average. (昌記; 📞852 2573 5910; 2nd fl, Wong Nai Chung Market & Cooked Food Centre, 2 Yuk Sau St, Happy Valley; meals from HK$30; ⏱7am-4.30pm; 🚌1 from Des Voeux Rd Central, 🚋Happy Valley)

Samsen
THAI $$

18 MAP P92, D4

One bite of Samsen's delectable pad thai and Queen's Rd East

Caroline Haven

The old, middle-class neighbourhood bound roughly by Caroline Hill Rd, Haven St, and the eastern section of Leighton Rd has become a haven for independents exiled by the rocketing rents of Causeway Bay. It centres around a '60s residential block and its time-forgotten arcades with multiple entrances threading through the ground floor. At the corner of Leighton Rd and Caroline Hill Rd, you'll spot (or smell) **Danish Bakery** (Ground Fl, Morrison Bldg, 106 Leighton Rd, Causeway Bay), which has been slinging greasy burgers and fried chicken legs for four decades. Inside the arcades and along their peripheries, a smattering of trendy bars, boutiques and restaurants have taken root alongside *cha chaan tangs* and eccentric speciality shops.

STRIPPED PIXEL / SHUTTERSTOCK ©

Squid ink spaghetti at Tung Po Seafood Restaurant

becomes Khao San Rd; but at this hip little gem presided over by an Aussie chef, the good ol' backpacker staple is pimped up with plump tiger prawns, paired with zingy Thai salads and washed down with Moonzen craft beer. Expect to queue. (泰麵; ☏852 2234 0001; 68 Stone Nullah Lane, Wan Chai; dishes from HK$118; ⏰noon-2.30pm & 6.30-11pm; Ⓜ Wan Chai, exit D)

Seventh Son   CANTONESE $$

19 ⓧ MAP P92, C3

Worthy spin-off from the illustrious and famously wallet-unfriendly Fook Lam Moon (p136; aka Tycoon's Canteen, for its clientele of movie stars and politicians), Seventh Son reproduces to a T FLM's home-style dishes and a few extravagant seafood numbers as well.

The food here is excellent, prices are fair, plus you get the treatment FLM reserves for regulars. (家全七福; ☏852 2892 2888; www.seventhson.hk; 3rd fl, Wharney Guangdong Hotel, 57-73 Lockhart Rd, Wan Chai; meals from HK$350; ⏰11.30am-3pm & 6-10.30pm; Ⓜ Wan Chai, exit C)

Kam's Kitchen   CANTONESE $$

20 ⓧ MAP P92, H2

A family feud at the venerable Yung Kee in Central created this excellent-value spin-off. Kam's Kitchen serves classic, labour-intensive Cantonese dishes like prawn stuffed with crab roe and oysters sizzling with ginger and onion. And, of course, the famous goose is still here, as a roasted bird or with its fat drizzled into fried rice. (甘飯館; ☏852 3568

2832; 5 Mercury St, Tin Hau; lunch HK$60-300, dinner from HK$200; ⊙11.30am-3pm & 6-10.30pm; Ⓜ Tin Hau, exit A1)

Tung Po Seafood Restaurant
MARKET, CANTONESE $$

21 Ⓧ MAP P92, H1

You're guaranteed a hearty repast at any *dai pai dong* atop Java Rd Wet Market, but at Tung Po (and its sister spot, 店小二), you'll discover fusion Cantonese with a higher price tag and a dash of eccentricity. Thursday to Saturday, it's Hong Kong's most riotous dinner, as bowls of beer are downed to blaring '90s R & B. (東寶小館; ☎852 2880 5224, 852 2880 9399; 2nd fl, Java Rd Wet Market, Municipal Services Bldg, 99 Java Rd, North Point; meals HK$200-600; ⊙5.30pm-midnight; Ⓜ North Point, exit A1)

Liu Yuan Pavilion
SHANGHAI $$

22 Ⓧ MAP P92, C4

This bright, pleasant restaurant in airy yellows makes superb Shanghainese classics, from *xiao long bao* (soup dumplings) with crabmeat to a jiggly, melt-in-your-mouth braised ham hock. It has a loyal following among the local Shanghainese community, so do book ahead. Sharing dishes and large tables suit groups. (留園雅款; ☎852 2804 2000; 3rd fl, The Broadway, 54-62 Lockhart Rd, Wan Chai; meals HK$200-600; ⊙noon-2.30pm & 6-10.30pm; Ⓜ Wan Chai, exit C)

Pawn Kitchen
BRITISH $$

23 Ⓧ MAP P92, C4

Occupying the 2nd floor of a historic balconied building, the Pawn impresses with modern British cooking: mussels steamed in malt beer with 'big chips', rustic fish pie and founding chef Tom Aiken's signature macaroni cheese with braised beef, lobster or truffle. Try to book an alfresco balcony table. (☎852 2866 3444; www.thepawn.com.hk; 62 Johnston Rd, Wan Chai; mains from HK$200; ⊙11am-2am Mon-Sat, to midnight Sun; Ⓜ Wan Chai, exit A3)

Hong Zhou Restaurant
ZHEJIANG $$

24 Ⓧ MAP P92, D4

A food critics' favourite, this establishment excels at Hángzhōu cooking, the delicate sister of Shanghainese cuisine. Dishes such as shrimp stir-fried with tea leaves show how the best culinary creations should engage all your senses. Its version of Dongpo pork (東坡肉), a succulent braised pork-belly dish named after a gluttonous poet, is cholesterol heaven. (杭州酒家; ☎852 2591 1898; 1st fl, Chinachem Johnston Plaza, 178-186 Johnston Rd, Wan Chai; meals HK$200-800; ⊙11.30am-2.30pm & 5.30-10.30pm; Ⓜ Wan Chai, exit A5)

Bo Innovation
CHINESE $$$

Committed foodies with dollars to burn will be determined to try this three-starred gastro-lab (see **23** Ⓧ Map p92, C4) presided over by the

'Demon Chef', aka Hong Kong's own Alvin Leung. Celebrated for his self-styled 'X-Treme Cuisine', Leung rips up the rule book and re-imagines Chinese classics in bold and often outrageous ways. (廚魔; 📞852 2850 8371; www.boinnovation. com; 1st fl, 60 Johnston Rd, Wan Chai; lunch set HK$750, tasting menu HK$900, dinner tasting menu HK$2280-2680; ⏰noon-2pm Mon-Fri, 7-10pm Mon-Sat; Ⓜ Wan Chai, exit B2)

Yee Tung Heen
DIM SUM, CANTONESE $$$

25 ✖ MAP P92, F3

This elegant and underhyped restaurant is an expert at haute Cantonese cuisine. Managed by the Mandarin Oriental, it delivers MO-quality food and service at two-thirds of the price; it's easier to book too. The best ingredients are painstakingly prepared and pre-sented to impress, as exemplified by lunchtime dim sum offerings such as eggplant pastry and the award-winning mushroom assort-ment. (怡東軒; 📞852 2837 6790; 2nd fl, Excelsior Hotel, 281 Gloucester Rd, Causeway Bay; lunch/dinner from HK$200/500; ⏰noon-3pm & 6-10pm; Ⓜ Causeway Bay, exit D1)

Forum
CANTONESE, DIM SUM $$$

26 ✖ MAP P92, F3

The flagship of a fine-dining brand with over a dozen branches worldwide, this two-Michelin-star eatery serves exquisite Guǎngdōng classics (including lunchtime dim sum). But Forum is most renowned for its braised abalone prepared from a recipe by the award-winning chef-owner Yeung Koon-yat. The bad news: it starts at HK$2100 (cheaper with the set menu, but you'll need six diners). (富臨飯店阿一鮑魚; Ah Yat Abalone; 📞852 2869 8282; www.forumrestaurant1977.com; 1st fl, Sino Plaza, 255-257 Jaffe Rd, Causeway Bay; meals HK$500-1600; ⏰11am-2.30pm & 5.30-10.30pm; Ⓜ Causeway Bay, exit D4)

Drinking

Second Draft
CRAFT BEER

27 🍺 MAP P92, H3

Tall windows wrap around a magisterial sweep of wooden bar at this Tai Hang neighbourhood gastropub, the sort of civilised joint where everybody knows everybody. A curated line-up of local beers favours the faultless Young Master brewery (450mL pours around HK$80), or go for an organic wine, paired with creative nibbles such as edamame with crispy chicken skin. (📞852 2656 0232; 98 Tung Lo Wan Rd, Tin Hau; ⏰noon-1am; Ⓜ Tin Hau, exit B)

Skye Bar
BAR

28 🍺 MAP P92, G3

The views are to die for at this open-air rooftop gem jutting out from the corner of the Park Lane Hotel. Treat yourself to a glass of Perrier-Jouët champers (HK$170) at the curvaceously sociable bar as you drink in one of the most magnificent harbour panoramas in the city. Ah, Hong Kong. (☎852 2839 3327; 22nd fl, Park Lane Hotel, 10 Gloucester Rd, Causeway Bay; ⊘noon-1am; ⓂCauseway Bay, exit E)

Botanicals
BAR

On the 1st floor of gorgeous heritage pile the Pawn (see **23** ✖ Map p92, C4), Botanicals draws after-work imbibers to its stylish twin bars and colonial-chic verandah for wines by the glass, craft beers and playful cocktails (after 5pm) including 10-cask negronis (HK$100 to HK$140) concocted from a variety of gin infusions, boutique vermouths and herbal additions. (☎852 2866 3444; www.thepawn.com. hk; 1st fl, 62 Johnston Rd, Wan Chai; ⊘11.30am-1am Sun-Thu, to 2am Fri & Sat; ⓂWan Chai, exit A3)

Stone Nullah Tavern
BAR

29 🚇 MA P P92, D4

The Americana theme is downplayed at this corner tavern that packs in punters for Wan Chai's best happy hour – unlimited house spirits, wines, Pabst Blue Ribbon beer, fried chicken and maple bacon (5pm to 7pm, HK$100). The rest of the time, it's a convivial hang-out for well-mixed cocktails (HK$99), bourbon or Young Master craft beer in a hip, historic neighbourhood. (☎852 3182 0128; www.stonenullahtavern.com; 69 Stone Nullah Lane, Wan Chai; ⊘noon-1am; ⓂWan Chai, exit A3)

Dim sum in bamboo steamers

Executive Bar

LOUNGE

30 🗺 MAP P92, F4

There are just 20 seats at this discreet gem of a bar overlooking the racecourse, which means Japanese owner and bartender Ichiro (it's a one-man operation) can give you his undivided attention. Perfectionist spins on classic cocktails employ fresh fruits imported from Japan, hand-chipped ice and house-infused bitters that change with the seasons. Ichiro has a terrific whisky selection too. (852 2893 2080; http://executivebar-com-hk-1.blogspot.hk; 27th fl, Bartlock Centre, 3 Yiu Wa St, Causeway Bay; ⏰5.30pm-1am Mon-Fri, to 2am Sat; M Causeway Bay, exit A)

Sugar

LOUNGE

31 🗺 MAP P92, H1

Enviable East Island views are the drawcard at this stylish terrace bar atop designer business hotel East (香港東隅; www.east-hongkong. com). With signature peach mojito in hand, take in the prosperity: the glass towers of Taikoo Pl to the west, the Kai Tak cruise terminal (formerly the old airport runway) in the bay in front. Reserve a table for Thursday to Saturday evenings. (852 3968 3738; www.east-hongkong. com/en/restaurants-and-bars/sugar; 32nd fl, East Hotel, 29 Taikoo Sing Rd, Quarry Bay; ⏰5.30pm-1am Mon-Thu & Sun, to 1.30am Fri & Sat; M Tai Koo, exit D1)

Hong Kong Island Taphouse

CRAFT BEER

32 🗺 MAP P92, H2

A dazzling chrome cliff face of around 50 taps showcases Hong Kong beers from Young Master, Moonzen, Kowloon Bay, Lion Rock, Gweilo, Mak's and more at this sporty neighbourhood bar. You'll pay around HK$80 for a 400mL pour. The kitchen turns out respectably lip-smacking wings, too, slathered in a choice of 10 sauces. (852 3705 9901; 1A-1B Tsing Fung St, Tin Hau; ⏰1pm-2am; M Tin Hau, exit A2)

Manson's Lot

CAFE

33 🗺 MAP P92, C4

Impeccable Australian-roasted coffee is the draw at this pretty little boho cafe popular for its lunch sets. Some relevant trivia as you enjoy your flat white – in the 19th century, the ground under you belonged to the founder of Hong Kong's first dairy farm, a Scottish surgeon called Patrick Manson. (852 2362 1899; www.mansonslot.com; 15 Swatow St, Wan Chai; ⏰8am-6.30pm, to 8pm Thu-Sat; M Wan Chai, exit D)

Entertainment

Hong Kong Academy for the Performing Arts

DANCE, THEATRE

34 ⭐ MAP P92, C3

With its striking triangular atrium and an exterior Meccano-like frame (a work of art in itself), the APA (1985) is a Wan Chai landmark

Shopping

Happy Valley Racecourse

An outing at the races is one of the quintessential Hong Kong things to do, especially if you're around during the weekly Wednesday-evening races. Punters pack into the stands and trackside, with branded beer stalls, silly wigs and live music setting up an electric party atmosphere.

To bet, you must first exchange cash for betting vouchers inside the stands, then use the machine terminals (which have English settings and instructions). Stewards will help. The first horse races were held here way back in 1846. Now meetings are held both here and at the newer and larger (but less atmospheric) **Sha Tin Racecourse** (沙田賽馬場; www.hkjc.com; Penfold Park, Sha Tin; race-day public stands HK$10, members' enclosures HK$100-150; M Racecourse) in the New Territories. Check the website for details on betting and tourist packages. Take the eastbound Happy Valley tram to the final stop and cross the road to the racecourse. You can use an Octopus card to enter the turnstiles. (跑馬地馬場; ☎852 2895 1523; www.hkjc.com/home/english/index.asp; 2 Sports Rd, Happy Valley; HK$10; ⏰7-10.30pm Wed Sep-Jun; 🚋Happy Valley)

and a major performance venue for music, dance, theatre and scholarship. Check out its online event calendar for exhibits and performances. (香港演藝學院; ☎852 2584 8500; www.hkapa.edu; 1 Gloucester Rd, Wan Chai; M Admiralty, exit E2)

Wanch   LIVE MUSIC

35 ⭐ MAP P92, C3

Decked out in old Hong Kong paraphernalia, the Wanch, so called for Wan Chai district's nickname, has live music (mostly classic rock, blues and folk) nightly from 9.30pm. Jam night is Monday from 8pm. There's no cover charge. Happy hour is 5pm to 9pm. (☎852 2861 1621; www.thewanch.hk; 54 Jaffe Rd, Wan Chai; M Wan Chai, exit C)

Shopping

Fashion Walk   CLOTHING

36 🅐 MAP P92, G3

A mostly street-level fashion-shopping mecca spanning four streets in Causeway Bay – Paterson, Cleveland, Great George and Kingston. It's where you'll find big names such as Comme des Garcons, Sandro and Kiehl's, but also high-street favourites, up-and-coming local brands and shops with off-the-rack high-street labels. (www.fashionwalk.com.hk; ⏰office 10am-11pm; M Causeway Bay, exit D4)

Wan Chai's Markets

The area sandwiched by Queen's Rd East and Johnston Rd in Wan Chai is a lively outdoor bazaar thronged with vendors, shoppers and parked cars. Cross St and Wan Chai Rd feature **wet markets** (灣仔街市; Map p92, D4; Zenith, 258 Queen's Rd E, Wan Chai; ⏰6am-8pm; Ⓜ Wan Chai, exit A3) in all their screaming splendour. **Tai Yuen Street** (Map p92, C4; Tai Yuen St, Wan Chai; ⏰10am-7.30pm; Ⓜ Wan Chai, exit A3), aka 'toy street' (玩具街; *woon gui kaai*) to locals, has hawkers selling goldfish, plastic flowers and granny underwear, but it's best known for a dwindling number of traditional toy shops, where you'll find not only kiddies' playthings, but clockwork tin and other kidult collectibles. Spring Garden Lane and Wan Chai Rd are a treasure trove of quirky shops selling everything from spices to funerary offerings and electronic gadgets.

Kapok
FASHION & ACCESSORIES

37 🔒 MAP P92, B4

In the hip Star St area, this Hong Kong–born boutique stocks a fastidiously curated selection of luxe-cool menswear labels (plus their own, Future Classics), along with bags and quirky design gifts. A cafe counter means you can sip single-origin espresso as you browse. A more fashion-oriented sister boutique is around the corner at 5 St Francis Yard. (📞852 2549 9254; www.ka-pok.com; 3 Sun St, Wan Chai; ⏰11am-8pm, to 6pm Sun; Ⓜ Admiralty, exit F, Ⓜ Wan Chai, exit B1)

Pacific Place
MALL

38 🔒 MAP P92, A4

A polished marble sea of high-end couture and accessories, posh Pacific Place manages to avoid the malady of mall fatigue via its expansive design, relatively light footfall and skylights which let the natural light pour in. (太古廣場; 📞852 2844 8988; www.pacificplace.com.hk; 88 Queensway, Admiralty; ⏰10am-10pm; Ⓜ Admiralty, exit F)

Eslite
BOOKS

39 🔒 MAP P92, F3

You could waste hours inside this swanky three-floor Taiwanese bookshop, which features a massive collection of English and Chinese books and magazines, a shop selling gorgeous stationery and leather-bound journals, a cafe, a bubble-tea counter and a huge kids' toy and book section. (誠品; 📞852 3419 6789; 8th-10th fl, Hysan Pl, 500 Hennessy Rd, Causeway Bay; ⏰10am-10pm Sun-Thu, to 11pm Fri & Sat; 🚹; Ⓜ Causeway Bay, exit F2)

Times Square MALL

40 🔒 MAP P92, F3

The hyperkinetic buzz at the heart of Causeway Bay, Times Square is retail nirvana for Hong Kong's shoppers, with mainstream brands over 13 floors (it was the first 'vertical mall' in the city), restaurants, cafes, a cinema and the famous clock on the forecourt outside – like with its namesake in NYC, revellers congregate here on 31 December for the countdown. (時代廣場; www.timessquare.com.hk; 1 Matheson St, Causeway Bay; Ⓜ Causeway Bay, exit A)

Two Girls COSMETICS

41 🔒 MAP P92, F3

Hong Kong's first cosmetics brand has been selling fragrant, highly affordable creams, potions, perfumes and talcs since 1898. The pretty, retro packaging featuring two cheongsam-clad beauties makes these excellent gifts. (雙妹嚜; 🕿 862 2504 1811; www.twogirls.hk; Shop 283, 2-10 Great George St, Causeway Pl, Causeway Bay; Ⓩ noon-9pm; Ⓜ Causeway Bay, exit E)

Papabubble FOOD

42 🔒 MAP P92, H3

This Spanish artisan candy company's Hong Kong outpost sells unique-to-here flavours such as lemon tea and durian, featuring local designs like Chinese zodiac animals and the character for 'double happiness'. Great gifts. Kids will love watching the hot sugar being pulled behind the counter. (🕿 852 2367 4807; www.papabubble.com.hk; 34 Tung Lo Wan Rd, Tai Hang; Ⓩ 11am-10pm; 👬; Ⓜ Tin Hau, exit B)

Yiu Fung Store FOOD

43 🔒 MAP P92, F3

Now with several branches around town, Hong Kong's most famous store (c 1960s) for Chinese pickles and preserved fruit features sour plum, liquorice-flavoured lemon, tangerine peel, pickled papaya and dried longan. Just before the Lunar New Year, it's crammed with shoppers. (么鳳; 🕿 852 2576 2528; http://yiufungstore.hk; Foo Ming St, Causeway Bay; Ⓩ 11am-10.30pm; Ⓜ Causeway Bay, exit A)

Wan Chai Computer Centre ELECTRONICS

44 🔒 MAP P92, C4

Buy a drone, build a custom gaming PC, or repair the iPhone screen you cracked on that Lan Kwai Fong bar crawl. You can do it all and more at this gleaming, beeping warren of tiny electrical shops. (灣仔電腦城; 1st fl, Southorn Centre, 130-138 Hennessy Rd, Wan Chai; Ⓩ 10am-9pm Mon-Sat, noon-8pm Sun; Ⓜ Wan Chai, exit B1)

Explore ⊛

Aberdeen & South Hong Kong Island

This is Hong Kong Island's backyard playground, strung with beaches, home to Ocean Park, popular with shoppers at Stanley Market and Horizon Plaza. It's also a showcase of history – Pok Fu Lam has the island's last surviving village, and Aberdeen and Ap Lei Chau are the homes of Hong Kong's boat-dwelling fisherfolk.

The Short List

◦ **Aberdeen Promenade (p114)** *Watching the goings-on on moored boats then hopping on a sampan to cross the typhoon shelter the way it was done decades ago*

◦ **Ap Lei Chau Market Cooked Food Centre (p119)** *Gorging on seafood without busting a hole in your pocket*

◦ **Béthanie (p114)** *Revisiting a time in Hong Kong history when French missionaries crossed paths with dairy cowboys and a fire dragon in Pok Fu Lam*

◦ **Stanley (p114)** *Downing a pint or two at the British-style pubs in this seaside town and taking a dip at one of its beaches*

◦ **Dragon's Back (p115)** *Hiking the city's most famous trail*

Getting There & Around

Ⓜ The MTR South Island Line runs from Admiralty to South Horizons and Lei Tung (both Ap Lei Chau), Wong Chuk Hang and Ocean Park.

🚌 Stanley, Deep Water Bay: 6A, 6X and 260 from Central (below Exchange Sq).

🚌 Aberdeen: 73 and 973 from Stanley, bus 107 from Kowloon Bay, buses 90B and 91 from Pok Fu Lam.

Neighbourhood Map on p112

Deep Water Bay and Repulse Bay (p111) MOLLY BROWN NZ / SHUTTERSTOCK ©

Walking Tour 🥾

Beach-Hopping on Island South

Beach-hopping along the Island's southern coastline is fun and convenient. Lots of beaches have showers, and most have other sights and restaurants in the vicinity. In the summer the waters around Stanley and Repulse Bay teem with bioluminescent algae. Go after sundown to feel like you're swimming with fireflies.

Walk Facts

Start Deep Water Bay beach; 6A, 6X or 260 to Island Rd

End Stanley; bus 6 to Tung Tau Wan Rd

Length 6.5km, 4½ hours

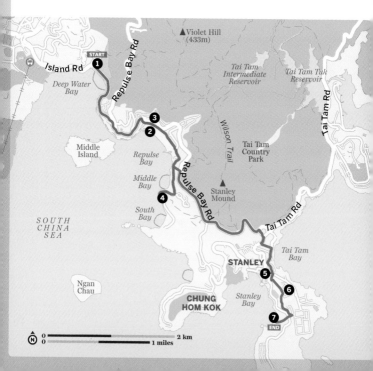

❶ Deep Water Bay

Start from the westernmost Deep Water Bay (深水灣), a quiet little inlet with a beach flanked by shade trees. Though not as famous as its neighbour Repulse Bay, it's less crowded and its barbecue pits are a real draw for locals – a dip here, especially in late afternoon, is sometimes accompanied by the tantalising aromas of grilled meat.

❷ Repulse Bay

From Deep Water Bay, walk 2km via the scenic Seaview Promenade to Repulse Bay (淺水灣). The long beach with tawny sand and murky water is packed almost all the time in summer. At its southeast end there's an assembly of deities and figures, all expressed in garish cartoon kitsch. The hills here are strewn with luxury residences.

❸ Verandah Restaurant

The elegant **Verandah** (露台餐廳; 📞852 2292 2822; www.therepulsebay. com; 1st fl, 109 Repulse Bay Rd, Repulse Bay; meals from HK$600) drips with colonial nostalgia, with its grand piano, marble staircase and wooden ceiling fans. The afternoon tea is the best this side of Hong Kong Island. Book ahead.

❹ Middle & South Bay

These attractive beaches are about a 10-minute and 30-minute walk to the south of Repulse Bay respectively. Middle Bay (淺水灣) is popular with gay beach goers, while French expats are drawn to South Bay (淺水灣). Swimming here on summer nights, you'll see specks of algae glowing like stars in the water.

❺ Stanley Market

No big bargains or big stings at this market (p114), just reasonably priced casual clothes (including big sizes and children's wear), bric-a-brac, souvenirs and formulaic art, all in a nicely confusing maze of alleys running down to Stanley Bay. It's best to go during the week when the market isn't bursting with tourists and locals.

❻ St Stephen's College

WWII history buffs should visit the beautiful campus of **St Stephen's College** (聖士反書院文物徑; www.ssc.edu.hk/ssctrail/eng; 22 Tung Tau Wan Rd, Stanley; admission free), which sits next to Stanley Military Cemetery, southeast of Stanley Market. Founded in 1903, the school was turned into an emergency military hospital on the eve of the Japanese invasion of Hong Kong in 1941 and became an internment camp after the city fell. Admission is by a two-hour guided tour only – reserve in advance via the website.

❼ St Stephen's Beach

This hidden **bolt-hole** (聖士提反灣泳灘) south of Stanley Village is cleaner than Stanley Main Beach, and there are windsurfing boards and kayaks for hire. Take the bus to Stanley then walk south along Wong Ma Kok Rd. Turn right into Wong Ma Kok Path, then turn south and go past the boathouse to the beach.

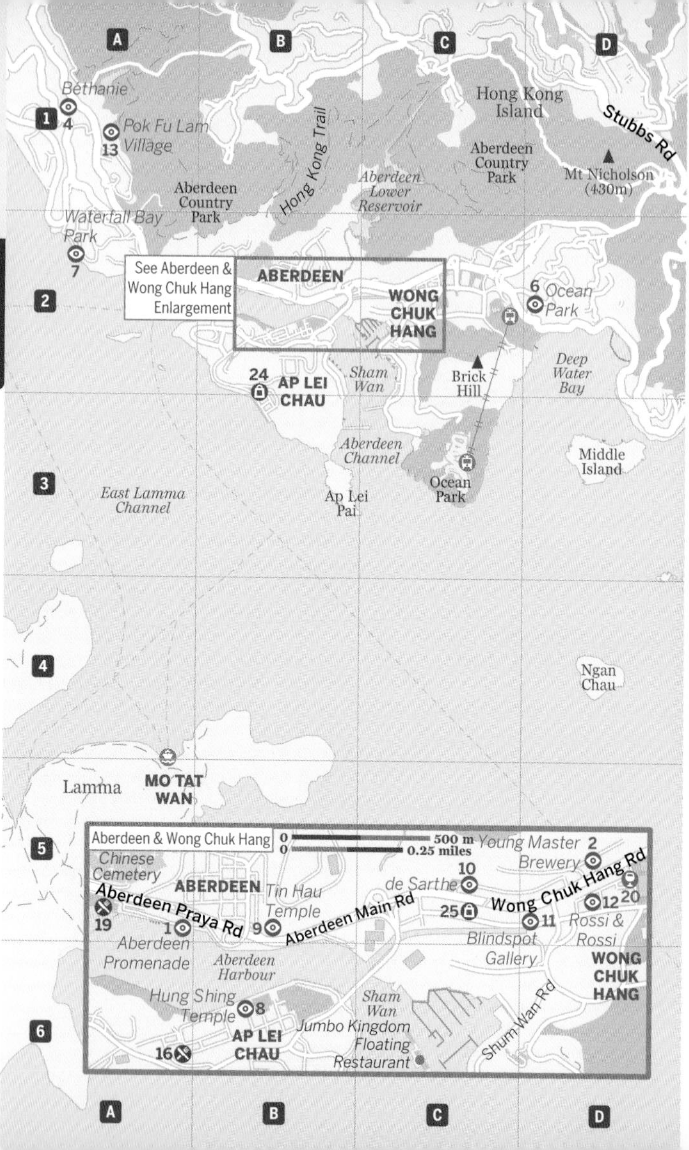

Bethanie
4
1
Pok Fu Lam
13 Village

Hong Kong Island

Hong Kong Trail

Aberdeen Lower Reservoir

Stubbs Rd

Aberdeen Country Park

Aberdeen Country Park

Mt Nicholson (430m)

Waterfall Bay Park
7

See Aberdeen & Wong Chuk Hang Enlargement

ABERDEEN

WONG CHUK HANG

6 Ocean Park

24 AP LEI CHAU

Sham Wan

Brick Hill

Deep Water Bay

East Lamma Channel

Aberdeen Channel

Ap Lei Pai

Ocean Park

Middle Island

Ngan Chau

Lamma

MO TAT WAN

Aberdeen & Wong Chuk Hang
0   500 m
0   0.25 miles

Young Master 2 Brewery

Chinese Cemetery

ABERDEEN

Tin Hau Temple

10
de Sarthe

Wong Chuk Hang Rd

Rossi & Rossi
12 20

Aberdeen Praya Rd
19
1 9

Aberdeen Main Rd

25

11

Blindspot Gallery

WONG CHUK HANG

Aberdeen Promenade

Aberdeen Harbour

Hung Shing Temple
8

Sham Wan

Jumbo Kingdom Floating Restaurant

Shum Wan Rd

AP LEI CHAU

16

Aberdeen & South Hong Kong Island

For reviews see

⊙ Sights	p114
✖ Eating	p119
🍷 Drinking	p120
🛍 Shopping	p120

E — Jardine's Lookout

Mt Butler (436m)

Tai Tam Country Park

Tai Tam Reservoir

Hong Kong Trail

Violet Hill (433m)

Shek O Country Park

Tai Tam Intermediate Reservoir

Wilson Trail

Tai Tam Tuk Reservoir

14

Dragon Back Trail

Big Wave Bay Rd

Tai Tam Waterworks Heritage Trail

Tai Tam Harbour

Shek O Peak (284m)

17

Repulse Bay

Repulse Bay Rd

Tai Tam Country Park

Stanley Mound (386m)

Tai Tam Rd

Shek O Rd

21

SHEK O

5

Shek O Beach

South Bay

Tai Tam Rd

STANLEY

See Stanley Enlargement

D'Aguilar Peak (323m)

CHUNG HOM KOK

Stanley Bay

Stanley

Carmel Rd

Stanley Main Beach

18

STANLEY

Hong Kong Aquabound Centre

23

22

3

15

Stanley Bay

Stanley

Wong Ma Kok Rd

0 ___ 400 m
0 ___ 0.2 miles

0 ___ 2 km
0 ___ 1 mile

Sights

Aberdeen Promenade

WATERFRONT

1 🎯 MAP P112, A5

Tree-lined Aberdeen Promenade runs from west to east on Aberdeen Praya Rd across the water from Ap Lei Chau. On its western end is sprawling **Aberdeen Wholesale Fish Market** (香港仔魚市場; 🚌70, 72, 72, Ⓜ Wong Chuk Hang, exit B) with its industrial-strength water tanks teeming with marine life. It's pungent and grimy, but 100% Hong Kong. Before reaching the market, you'll pass berthed house boats and seafood-processing vessels. (We detected a karaoke parlour or two as well.) (香港仔海濱公園; Aberdeen Praya Rd, Aberdeen; admission free; Ⓜ Wong Chuk Hang, exit B)

Young Master Brewery

BREWERY

2 🎯 MAP P112, D5

Young Master Ales has moved to a new street-level location in Wong Chuk Hang. Merchandise is sold in the front, while at the back, the brewing system, ageing barrels, and bottling line whir, hiss and grind away. The small-batch, nonfiltered, chemical-free beers range from crisp to robust, and have funky names inspired by Hong Kong pop culture – like fake blood, a tribute to kung fu movies. Book online for the Saturday hour-long guided tours (English 1pm, Cantonese 4pm). You cannot imbibe on the premises, but you can buy beer to take away. (少爺麥啤; www.youngmasterales.com; Ground fl, Sungib Industrial Centre, 53 Wong Chuk Hang Rd, Wong Chuk Hang; tour HK$100; 🕘9am-6pm Mon-Sat, closed Sun; Ⓜ Wong Chuk Hang, exit A2)

Stanley

VILLAGE

3 🎯 MAP P112, G6

This crowd-pleaser is best visited on weekdays. **Stanley Market** (赤柱市集; Stanley Village Rd, Stanley; 🕘9am-6pm; 🚌6, 6A, 6X, 260) is a maze of alleyways that has bargain clothing (haggling is a must!), while **Stanley Main Beach** (赤柱正灘; 🚌6A, 14) is for beach-bumming and windsurfing. With graves dating back to 1841, **Stanley Military Cemetery** (赤柱軍人墳場; ☎852 2557 3498; Wong Ma Kok Rd, Stanley; 🕘8am-5pm; 🚌14, 6A), 500m south of the market, is worth a visit.

Béthanie

HISTORIC BUILDING

4 🎯 MAP P112, A1

Perched on hilly Pok Fu Lam, a college and residential area northwest of Aberdeen, this beautiful restoration is a highlight in this part of town. The complex, which now houses a film school, was built by the French Mission in 1875 as a sanatorium for priests from all over Asia to rest and recover from tropical diseases before they returned to their missions. (伯大尼; ☎852 2584 8918; www.hkapa.edu/about/getting-here/; 139 Pok Fu Lam Rd, Pok Fu Lam; HK$25; 🕘11am-6pm

Mon-Sat, from noon Sun; 🚌7, 40, 40M, 90B, 91)

Shek O Beach BEACH

5 ◎ MAP P112, H3

Shek O beach has a large expanse of sand, shady trees to the rear, showers, changing facilities and lockers for rent. It's not quiet by any means, except on typhoon days, but the laid-back beach framed by rocky cliffs is quite pleasant. (石澳; 🚌9 from Shau Kei Wan MTR, exit A3)

Ocean Park AMUSEMENT PARK

6 ◎ MAP P112, D2

Despite the crowd-pulling powers of Disneyland on Lantau, Ocean Park remains the most popular theme park in Hong Kong. Constant expansion, new rides and thrills, and the presence of four giant pandas and two rare red pandas ensure the park remains a huge draw for families. Be aware that in part of the park, Marine World, cetaceans are kept in captivity and performances involving dolphins and orcas are a feature, which scientific studies suggest is harmful to these animals. Ocean Park is undergoing a mega expansion that will see the launch of the 3716-sq-metre Tai Shue Wan Water World in 2019/20. (海洋公園; ☎852 3923 2323; www.oceanpark.com.hk; Ocean Park Rd; adult/child 3-11yr HK$385/193; ⊙10am-7.30pm; 👪; Ⓜ Ocean Park)

Shek O beach

Waterfall Bay Park

PARK

7 ⊙ MAP P112, A2

The cascade and the bay here are serene and quite lovely. Barges and fishing junks streak the waters; Lamma is surprisingly near; figurines of gods – both Chinese and Hindu – stand on rocks. Overlooking the sea is a pillbox from WWII when British troops used Aberdeen as a bunker in the battle against the Japanese. The bay is also where the fire dragon of Pok Fu Lam village spectacularly enters the water in the finale of the Mid-Autumn Festival dance. (瀑布灣公園; Waterfall Bay Rd, Pok Fu Lam; 🚌4, 970, minibus 69)

Hung Shing Temple   TAOIST TEMPLE

8 ⊙ MAP P112, B6

Renovated many times since it was built in 1773 by local fishermen, Ap Lei Chau's major temple is dedicated to Hung Shing, the protector of seafarers. Its major features are a sea-facing orientation (which is believed to bring good feng shui), the fine Shiwan figurines on the roof ridges (which denote its significance), and the two timber 'dragon poles' in its forecourt, which are said to counter the 'death-like aura' of the Aberdeen Police Station across the water. (洪聖古廟; Hung Shing St; ⊙8am-5pm; Ⓜ Lei Tung, exit A1)

Tin Hau Temple

TEMPLE

9 ⊙ MAP P112, B5

Caught between a church and the thoroughfare, this temple has an eclectic deity collection, two moon gates and hovering incense coils. The stone columns, ridge ornaments featuring a legendary female warrior, and copper bell (rumoured to have been salvaged from the seabed by a fisher) are Qing dynasty, but the dragon-and-phoenix murals look decidedly 20th century. The temple worships the Goddess of the Sea, with nods to Wong Tai Sin, wish-granter extraordinaire. (天后廟; 182 Aberdeen Main Rd, Aberdeen; ⊙8am-5pm; 🚌70)

de Sarthe

GALLERY

10 ⊙ MAP P112, C5

The 900-sq-metre de Sarthe Gallery takes up the 20th floor of a new office block. The French gallery has exhibited an array of western and Asian artists, from French impressionists, and postwar artists, to contemporary and emerging talent. At the time of research, painter Lu Xinjian was presenting his paintings of metropolises in an exhibition entitled 'Boogie Woogie'. (☎852 2167 8896; www.desarthe.com/about.html; 20th fl, Global Trade Square, 21 Wong Chuk Hang Rd, Wong Chuk Hang; ⊙11am-7pm Tue-Sat; Ⓜ Wong Chuk Hang, exit A2)

Blindspot Gallery

GALLERY

11 MAP P112, D5

So named because the owner believed that contemporary photography was not getting the attention it deserved in Hong Kong, Blindspot Gallery features the works of photographers and artists from Hong Kong and Asia, including Stanley Wong, Ken Kitano and Maleonn. Arguably one of the best places to acquaint yourself with Hong Kong and Asian photography and video works. (刺點畫廊; ☎852 2517 6238; www. blindspotgallery.com; 15th fl, Po Chai Industrial Bldg, 28 Wong Chuk Hang Rd, Aberdeen; ◷10am-6pm Tue-Sat, by appointment only Sun & Mon; Ⓜ Wong Chuk Hang, exit A2)

Rossi & Rossi

GALLERY

12 MAP P112, D5

This gallery is founded by an Italian mother-and-son dealer duo and specialises in Asian art, in particular Indian, Himalayan and Southeast Asian, both classical and contemporary; Tibetan art is a forte. In response to the growing demand in Asia, the Rossis are branching into western art. (☎852 3575 9417; www.rossirossi.com; 3rd fl, unit C, Yally Industrial Bldg, 6 Yip Fat St, Wong Chuk Hang; ◷11am-6pm Tue-Sat; Ⓜ Wong Chuk Hang, exit A2)

Pok Fu Lam Village

VILLAGE

13 MAP P112, A1

Built on a sloping hillside, peaceful Pok Fu Lam Village looks like a shanty town compared to the high-density middle-class residences around it. Though no stunner, it's valued by historians not only for the famous fire dragon dance at the Mid-Autumn Festival, but equally for its ties to Hong Kong's dairy industry. Other highlights include Béthanie (p114) and Li Ling Pagoda. As the sites are scattered, the best way to see them all is to join a walking tour. Four-hour English tours are available upon request for about HK$700 per

Dragon's Back Trail

The city's most famous trail (龍脊) begins in a forest, soars to a mountain ridge evoking a dragon's spine, before dipping to fine sands and surf. Though Hong Kong has no shortage of visually and culturally superior trails, 8.5km Dragon's Back is relatively easy to access. And it is impressive. On days when the golf greens, the sea and the luxury homes are all gleaming in the sun, dotted with cloud shadow, it's downright surreal.

Bus 9 and minibuses with the 'Shek O' sign depart from Shau Kei Wan Bus Terminus, right next to exit A of Shau Kei Wan MTR station. Alight at the trailhead – To Tei Wan (土地灣) on Shek O Rd.

Sampan Tours

Sampan tours are a fun way to see parts of the island's south coast, and you can easily find sampan operators milling around the eastern end of the Aberdeen Promenade. Usually they charge around HK$60 to HK$80 per person for a 30-minute ride, around HK$160 to Sok Kwu Wan and around HK$170 to Yung Shue Wan on Lamma.

If you want just a glimpse of the harbour, you can take a small ferry across to Ap Lei Chau Island (adult/child under 12 HK$2.20/1.20) between 6am and midnight. Ap Lei Chau is also a destination for bargain hunters drawn to its outlet stores. Alternatively, just hop on the free ferry to **Jumbo Kingdom Floating Restaurant** (珍寶海鮮舫; Map p112, C6; ☎852 2553 9111; www.jumbo.com.hk; Shum Wan Pier Dr, Wong Chuk Hang; meals from HK$200; ⏱11am-11.30pm Mon-Sat, from 9am Sun; ✿ 👶; 🚌90 from Central, Ⓜ Wong Chuk Hang, exit B) and come back.

The promenade can be easily accessed from Aberdeen bus terminus or exit B of Wong Chuk Hang metro station. To get to it, just take the pedestrian subway under Aberdeen Praya Rd.

person. Email or call two weeks ahead to book. (薄扶林村; ☎Ms So 852 6199 9473; www.pflvarchives.org.hk; 🚌7, 40, 40M, 90B, 91)

Tai Tam Waterworks Heritage Trail
HIKING

14 ◉ MAP P112, F3

This scenic 5km trail runs past reservoirs and a handsome collection of 20 historic waterworks structures – feats of Victorian utilitarian engineering that include bridges, aqueducts, valve houses, pumping stations and dams, many still working. (大潭水務文物徑)

Hong Kong Aquabound Centre
WATER SPORTS

15 ◉ MAP P112, H5

You can rent kayaks, stand-up paddle boards, as well as equipment for windsurfing and wakeboarding at this place on Stanley Main Beach. You can also hire an instructor to teach you or your child. Prices vary according to class size. Make contact online to see rates, enquire for details or book. (☎852 8211 3876; www.aquabound.com.hk; Stanley Main Beach, Stanley; kayak rental per hr HK$80; ⏱9am-6.30pm; 🚌6A, 14)

Eating

Ap Lei Chau Market Cooked Food Centre
SEAFOOD $

16 ❌ MAP P112, A6

Above an indoor market, *dai pai dong* (food stall) operators cook up a storm in a sprawling hall littered with folding tables and plastic chairs. **Pak Kee** (栢記; ☎852 2555 2984; seafood meals from HK$160; ⏰6-10.30pm) and **Chu Kee** (珠記; ☎852 2555 2052; seafood meals from HK$180; ⏰6pm-midnight;) offer simple but tasty seafood dishes. You can also buy seafood from the wet market downstairs and pay for it to be cooked the way you want. It's packed and noisy on weekends. (鴨利洲市政大廈; 1st fl, Ap Lei Chau Municipal Services Bldg, 8 Hung Shing St, Ap Lei Chau; dishes HK$45-100; 🚌minibus 36X from Lee Garden Rd, Causeway Bay, Ⓜ Lei Tung, exit A1)

Amalfitana
PIZZA $

17 ❌ MAP P112, E3

Open frontage and its location a flip-flop's throw from the beach mean Amalfitana's delicious Italian-style pizzas can be enjoyed between dips in the water. Toppings are classic, with four 'bambino' versions for the little ones. You can order to take away too. (☎852 2388 7787; www.amalfitana.hk; Shop 105, Ground fl, The Pulse, 28 Beach Rd, Repulse Bay; pizzas HK$140-250; ⏰noon-10.30pm; ❄🍴👶; 🚌40, 90, 6X)

Sei Yik
CANTONESE $

18 ❌ MAP P112, H5

Weekenders flock to this small tin-roofed *dai pai dong*, right opposite the Stanley Municipal Building, for its fluffy Hong Kong–style French toast with *kaya* (coconut jam). There's no English sign; look for the long queue of pilgrims and the piles of fruits that hide the entrance. (泗益; ☎852 2813 0507; 2 Stanley Market St, Stanley; meals from HK$30; ⏰6am-4pm Wed-Mon; 🚌6, 6A, 6X, 66)

Aberdeen Fish Market Yee Hope Seafood Restaurant
CANTONESE, SEAFOOD $$

19 ❌ MAP P112, A5

Hidden in Hong Kong's only wholesale fish market, this understated eatery run by fishers is truly an in-the-know place for ultrafresh seafood. There's no menu, but tell them your budget and they'll source the best sea creatures available, including some not often seen in restaurants, and apply their Midas touch to them. (香港仔魚市場二合海鮮餐廳; ☎852 2177 7872, 852 5167 1819; 102 Shek Pai Wan Rd, Aberdeen; meals from HK$350; ⏰4am-2.30pm; 🚌107, Ⓜ Wong Chuk Hang, exit B)

Drinking

Komune
ROOFTOP BAR

20 🚻 MAP P112, D5

Komune serves beer, bubbles and cocktails, alongside Latin American– and Asian-inspired nibbles on the roof of the **Ovolo Southside** (Ovolo 南區; 📞852 2165 1000; www.ovolohotels.com; r HK$700-$1800). Sweeping views are a bonus. Happy hour is 3pm to 7pm. (www.komune.com.hk; 64 Wong Chuk Hang Rd; ⏰6.30am-11pm; 🚌73, 973, 42, 171, 99, Ⓜ Wong Chuk Hang, exit A2)

Ben's Back Beach Bar
BAR

21 🚻 MAP P112, H3

Hidden on Shek O's quiet back beach, Ben's is the neighbourhood watering hole where everyone knows everyone else. You'll find villagers, resident urbanites and expats sipping cold brews to reggae beats and the sound of the lapping waves. A sea-facing shrine stands next to this rugged ensemble. (石澳風帆會; 📞852 2809 2268; Shek O back beach, 273 Shek O Village; ⏰7pm-midnight Thu & Fri, from 11am Sat & Sun; 🚌9 from Shau Kei Wan MTR, exit A3)

Smugglers Inn
PUB

22 🚻 MAP P112, G6

When you're in an ever-renewing tourist hot spot like Stanley, it's nice to step into an institution like Smugglers Inn, where fads don't seem to have made an impact over the years. You can still have a Sex on the Beach next to its currency-plastered walls or outdoors on the waterfront, or play darts for free beers against fellow drinkers. There's even a jukebox. (📞852 2813 8852; Ground fl, 90A Stanley Main St, Stanley; ⏰10am-midnight Mon-Thu, to 1am Fri-Sun; 🚌6, 6A, 6X, 260)

Shopping

G.O.D.
CLOTHING, HOUSEWARES

23 🔒 MAP P112, G5

One of the coolest born in Hong Kong shops around, G.O.D. does irreverent takes on classic Hong Kong iconography. Think mobile-phone covers printed with pictures of Hong Kong housing blocks, light fixtures resembling the ones in old-fashioned wet markets, and pillows covered in lucky koi print. There are a handful of G.O.D. shops in town, but this is one of the biggest. (Goods of Desire; 📞852 2673 0071; www.god.com.hk; Shop 105, Stanley Plaza, 22-23 Carmel Rd, Stanley; ⏰10.30am-8pm Mon-Fri, to 9pm Sat & Sun; 🚌6, 6A, 6X, 260)

Horizon Plaza
MALL

24 🔒 MAP P112, B2

Tucked away on the southern coast of Ap Lei Chau, this enormous outlet housed in a converted factory building contains 100 shops over 25 storeys. Most locals come here to buy furniture, but you'll also find Alexander McQueen on offer and Jimmy Choos at knock-down prices. Heaps of kid-

Aberdeen's Fisherfolk Culture

Aberdeen Typhoon Shelter has long been part of the western imagination of Hong Kong, having appeared in numerous films including *Lara Croft: Tomb Raider 2*. It's where the sampans of the boat-dwelling fisherfolk used to moor.

In 1961, the population living in houseboats here stood at 28,000. Now only a few hundred remain.

There are under 2000 fishing junks left in Aberdeen. For many years, stable and better-paying jobs on land have lured younger fishermen away from their traditional engagement. Despite this, the majority of inhabitants in Aberdeen and Ap Lei Chau still see themselves as 'people of the water'. Each year this identity is flaunted with fanfare at dragon boat races held throughout the territory. On weekday evenings, you may see dragon boat teams practising in the typhoon shelter or chilling in Ap Lei Chau Market Cooked Food Centre (p119). Dragon boat racing, which started 2000 years ago in China as a ritual for worshipping water deities, was practised by fishermen but is now embraced as a sport by the whole city. Hong Kong is the home of modern dragon boat racing. The most spectacular events during the racing season (March to October) are the fishermen's races. The Dragon Boat Association (www.hkdba.com.hk) and Hong Kong Tourist Board (www.discoverhongkong.com) have listings.

dies' stuff as well, from books and toys to clothing and furniture. (新海怡廣場; www.horizonplazahk.com; 2 Lee Wing St, Ap Lei Chau; ⏱10am-7pm; Ⓜ South Horizons, exit C)

Edit x Editecture   CLOTHING

25 🔒 MAP P112, C5

This large office-shop-showroom belongs to two friends who have won awards designing everything from restaurants to clothes. The highlight here is the edgy streetwear under the house brand, Edit. The shop also has a library and hosts design events. A space to watch. (📞852 2548 8682; www.editecture.com; 10F, Unit B, Shui Ki Industrial Bldg, 18 Wong Chuk Hang Rd, Wong Chuk Hang)

Explore

Tsim Sha Tsui

Tsim Sha Tsui is endowed with marvellous museums, an unbeatable harbour setting and all the superlatives Central has to offer on a more human scale. Other assets include leafy parks, colonial gems and the most diverse ethnic mix in all of Hong Kong.

The Short List

○ **Symphony of Lights (p125)** *Seeing the Hong Kong skyline ablaze at this nightly light show*

○ **Peninsula (p131)** *Enjoying scones and a cup of Earl Grey in the palatial lobby of the 'Pen'*

○ **New Chettinad (p133)** *Trying Kowloon's famed ethnic cuisine*

○ **Kowloon Park (p130)** *Enjoying a breath of fresh air away from the Nathan Rd hustle*

○ **InterContinental Lobby Lounge (p137)** *Wrapping up your day with harbour-view drinks*

Getting There & Around

⚓ For Macau Ferries, the China Ferry Terminal is on Canton Rd (Tsim Sha Tsui). Star Ferries leave from the Star Ferry Pier at the western end of Salisbury Rd.

Ⓜ The Tsuen Wan Line goes north from Tsim Sha Tsui, with stops serving many of Kowloon's major markets and sights.

🚌 Buses leave from the Star Ferry Bus Terminal for points across Kowloon, Hong Kong Island and the New Territories. Useful routes include N21 (airport), 5A (Kowloon City) and 8 (Kowloon Station).

Neighbourhood Map on p128

The Peninsula Hong Kong (p131) RICHARD I'ANSON / GETTY IMAGES ©

Top Sight 📷
Tsim Sha Tsui East Promenade

Revamped with a new design in 2019, this walkway is once again one of the best strolls in Hong Kong, offering resplendent views of Victoria Harbour. Go during the day to take pictures and visit the museums. Then after sundown, revisit the views, now magically transformed, with the skyscrapers of Central and Wan Chai decked out in neon robes.

◎ MAP P128, F6

尖沙嘴東部海濱花園

Salisbury Rd, Tsim Sha Tsui

Ⓜ East Tsim Sha Tsui, exit J

Former KCR Clock Tower

A good place to begin your journey is at the **Former Kowloon-Canton Railway (KCR) Clock Tower** (前九廣鐵路鐘樓; Tsim Sha Tsui Star Ferry Concourse, Tsim Sha Tsui; 🚢 Star Ferry, Ⓜ East Tsim Sha Tsui, exit L6), a landmark of the age of steam, near the Star Ferry Concourse. In 1966 thousands gathered here to protest against a fare increase. The protest erupted into the 1966 riot, the first in a series of social protests leading to colonial reform.

Avenue of the Stars

A highlight of the newly renovated walkway is the revamped **Avenue of Stars** (星光大道; Tsim Sha Tsui East Promenade, Tsim Sha Tsui), just past the Cultural Centre and the Museum of Art. Hong Kong's tribute to its once-brilliant film industry, the highlight here is a 2.5m tall bronze statue of kung fu icon Bruce Lee.

Symphony of Lights

Every evening at 8pm you can watch the Symphony of Lights from the promenade, the world's largest permanent laser light show projected from atop dozens of skyscrapers. The show is set to music by the Hong Kong Philharmonic Orchestra, piped from speakers at the **Hong Kong Cultural Centre** (香港文化中心; www.lcsd.gov.hk; 10 Salisbury Rd, Tsim Sha Tsui; ⏰ 9am-11pm; 📶; Ⓜ East Tsim Sha Tsui, exit L6).

Tsim Sha Tsui East & Beyond

The walk takes you past the hotels of the reclaimed area known as Tsim Sha Tsui East, and past that to the **Hong Kong Coliseum** and the Hung Hom train station. The further north you go, the quieter it gets, and tourists and pleasure boats are replaced by container barges and men angling for fish.

★ Top Tips

o The waterfront has few dining options, so eat beforehand.

o Stroll eastward towards the Hong Kong Museum of History (p130), or visit the Hong Kong Science Museum (p130) if you have kids.

o Stake out a spot early if you want to catch the Chinese New Year fireworks (January to February) or June's Dragon Boat Festival.

✕ Take a Break

Stop for a coffee or cocktail with million-dollar views at the InterContinental Lobby Lounge (p137).

If you make it all the way to Tung Ho, reward yourself with snacks and cocktails at **Red Sugar** the rooftop bar at **Kerry Hotel** (香港嘉里酒店; 📞 852 2252 5888; www.shangri-la.com/hongkong/kerry; 38 Hung Luen Rd, Hung Hom).

Walking Tour 🚶

Vestiges of Local & Colonial Life in Tsim Sha Tsui

Tsim Sha Tsui's lesser-known northern end is a treasure trove of postwar buildings and colonial relics: behind the glam harbour-facing facade, churches and Shanghainese immigrant landmarks show just how eclectic Kowloon's heritage is – particularly around Austin and Nathan Rds.

Walk Facts

Start Former Kowloon British School

End Kowloon Union Church

Length 2.5km; 1½ hours

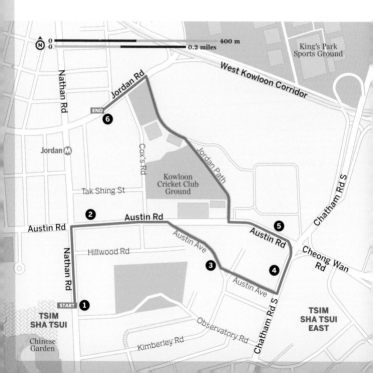

❶ Former Kowloon British School

Start your journey at the **Former Kowloon British School** (前九龍英童學校; www.amo.gov.hk; 136 Nathan Rd; Ⓜ Tsim Sha Tsui, exit B1) and **St Andrew's Anglican Church**, respectively Kowloon's oldest 'international' school and Anglican church. The former school now houses the Antiquities & Monuments Office (古物古蹟辦事處), which has information and exhibits on current efforts towards the preservation of traditional Chinese and colonial architecture.

❷ Pak On Building

Further north on Nathan Rd, turn right into Austin Rd, a former stronghold of Shanghainese migrants. Explore Pak On Building, with its lobby full of little shops, including, at the Tak Shing St end, a liquor store that stocks absinthe, among other tipples.

❸ Carnival Mansion

Make your way back to Austin Rd. At number 15 stands Carnival Mansion. Here a vortex of rickety postwar homes hangs above the courtyard and buildings have terrazzo staircases with green balustrades made by Shanghainese craftspeople 50 years ago. Enter at 15B for a peek into the vertigo-inducing inner courtyard. Opposite, you'll see the curious triangular public toilet, which doubles as a power substation.

❹ Rosary Church

Continue down Austin Ave and make a left on Chatham Rd South to find **Rosary Church** (玫瑰堂; http://rosarychurch.catholic.org.hk; 125 Chatham Rd S; ⊙ 7.30am-7.30pm). Reminiscent of churches in Macau, Kowloon's oldest Catholic church was built in 1905 with money donated by a Portuguese doctor in Hong Kong. It was initially intended for the benefit of the Catholics in an Indian battalion stationed in Kowloon, and later for the burgeoning local Catholic community. Next to it stands **St Mary's Canossian College**, built in 1900.

❺ People's Liberation Army Buildings

Turn left back up Austin Rd. At the cannon-guarded gate of **Gun Club Hill Barracks**, formerly used by the British and now occupied by the Chinese People's Liberation Army, turn right into leafy Jordan Path. The manicured lawns of the colonial recreation clubs unfurl on your left. Just before Jordan Rd, you'll see the **People's Liberation Army Hospital** with its darkened windows, constructed in 1997.

❻ Kowloon Union Church

Crossing Cox's Rd takes you to the Victorian-style Anglican **Kowloon Union Church** (九龍佑寧堂; www.kuc.hk; 4 Jordan Rd; ⊙ 9am-5pm Mon-Fri). It was built in 1930 in a neo-Gothic style – quite unusual for Kowloon – and features a Chinese-tiled pitched roof, which makes it typhoon-proof. Services are held here on Sundays at 10.30am.

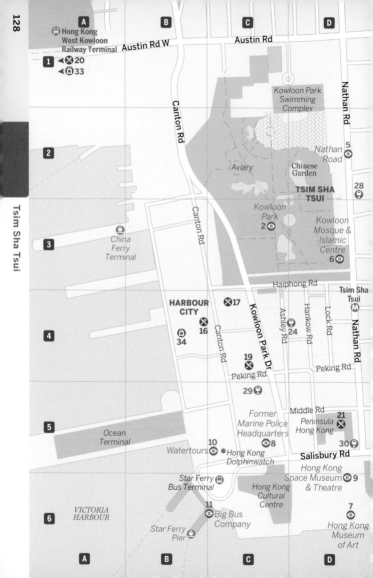

Hong Kong West Kowloon Railway Terminal

Austin Rd W

Austin Rd

1 ◀ ⊗ 20
◀ ⊕ 33

Canton Rd

Kowloon Park Swimming Complex

Nathan Rd

2

Nathan Road 5 ◉

Aviary

Chinese Garden

28 ◉

China Ferry Terminal

Canton Rd

Kowloon Park 2 ◉

TSIM SHA TSUI

Kowloon Mosque & Islamic Centre 6 ◉

3

Haiphong Rd

Tsim Sha Tsui Ⓜ

HARBOUR CITY

⊗ 17

⊗ 16

⊕ 24

4

⊕ 34

Canton Rd

Kowloon Park Dr

Ashley Rd

Hankow Rd

Lock Rd

Nathan Rd

⊗ 19

Peking Rd

Peking Rd

29 ⊕

Former Marine Police Headquarters

Middle Rd

Peninsula Hong Kong

21 ⊗

5

Ocean Terminal

10 ◉

Watertours ◉ ● Hong Kong Dolphinwatch

◉ 8

30 ⊕

Salisbury Rd

Hong Kong Space Museum ◉ 9 & Theatre

Star Ferry Bus Terminal

Hong Kong Cultural Centre

7 ◉

6

VICTORIA HARBOUR

11 ◉ Big Bus Company

Star Ferry Pier

Hong Kong Museum of Art

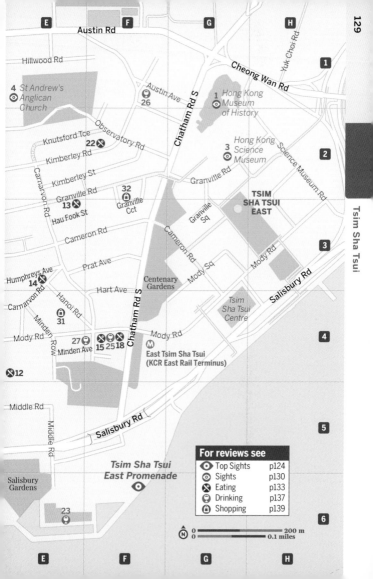

Tsim Sha Tsui

Austin Rd

Hillwood Rd

Cheong Wan Rd

Yuk Choi Rd

4 St Andrew's
Anglican
Church

Austin Ave
26

1 Hong Kong
Museum
of History

Knutsford Tce

Observatory Rd

3 Hong Kong
Science
Museum

Science Museum Rd

22

Kimberley Rd

Kimberley St

Chatham Rd S

Granville Rd

**TSIM
SHA TSUI
EAST**

Granville Rd

32
Granville
Cct

13

Carnarvon Rd

Hau Fook St

Granville Sq

Cameron Rd

Cameron Rd

Mody Rd

Prat Ave

Mody Sq

Humphreys Ave

14

Hart Ave

Centenary
Gardens

Salisbury Rd

Carnarvon Rd

Hanoi Rd

Tsim
Sha Tsui
Centre

Minden Row

31

Mody Rd

Minden Ave

27

15 25 18

Mody Rd

Chatham Rd S

M East Tsim Sha Tsui
(KCR East Rail Terminus)

12

Middle Rd

Middle Rd

Salisbury Rd

Salisbury
Gardens

**Tsim Sha Tsui
East Promenade**

23

For reviews see	
⊙ Top Sights	p124
⊙ Sights	p130
⊗ Eating	p133
⊖ Drinking	p137
🔒 Shopping	p139

Ⓝ 0 _____ 200 m
   0 _____ 0.1 miles

E   F   G   H

Sights

Hong Kong Museum of History

MUSEUM

1 ◎ MAP P128, G1

Prepare to be whisked through millennia of Hong Kong history at this extraordinary museum, starting with prehistory (don't linger, the best is yet to come) and ending with the territory's return to China in 1997. Highlights of the 'Hong Kong Story' include a recreation of an entire arcaded street in Central from 1881, a full-sized fishing junk, lots of informative video theatre exhibits (including an even-handed stab at the Opium Wars) – and so much more. (香港歷史博物館; ☏852 2724 9042; http://hk.history. museum; 100 Chatham Rd S, Tsim Sha Tsui; admission free; ⊙10am-6pm Mon & Wed-Sat, to 7pm Sun; ♿; Ⓜ Tsim Sha Tsui, exit B2)

Kowloon Park

PARK

2 ◎ MAP P128, C3

Built on the site of a barracks for an Indian regiment of the British Army, Kowloon Park is an oasis of greenery and a refreshing escape from the Nathan Rd hustle. Pathways wind between banyan trees, gardens, fountains and a flamingo pond; go early to see elderly locals performing taichi. (九龍公園; www. lcsd.gov.hk; Nathan & Austin Rds, Tsim Sha Tsui; ⊙6am-midnight; ♿; Ⓜ Tsim Sha Tsui, exit C2)

Hong Kong Science Museum

MUSEUM

3 ◎ MAP P128, G2

Younger kids will go wild for the vast array of hands-on exhibits at this modern museum. The boring old laws of physics, chemistry and biology are entertainingly presented via robots, VR, video games and more, along with traditional museum displays like model vehicles and dinosaur skeletons. (香港科學館; ☏852 2732 3232; http://hk.science.museum; 2 Science Museum Rd, Tsim Sha Tsui; adult/concession HK$25/12.50, Wed free; ⊙10am-7pm Mon-Wed & Fri, to 9pm Sat & Sun; ♿; Ⓜ Tsim Sha Tsui, exit B2)

St Andrew's Anglican Church

CHURCH

4 ◎ MAP P128, E1

Sitting atop a knoll adjacent to the Former Kowloon British School is this charming building in English Gothic style that houses Kowloon's oldest Protestant church. St Andrew's was built in 1905 in granite and red brick to serve Kowloon's Protestant population; it was turned into a Shinto shrine during the Japanese Occupation. Nearby you'll see the handsome **Old Vicarage** with its columned balconies (c 1909). Enter from the eastern side of Nathan Rd via steps or a slope. (聖安德烈堂; ☏852 2367 1478; www.standrews. org.hk; 138 Nathan Rd, Tsim Sha Tsui; ⊙7.30am-10.30pm, church 8.30am-5.30pm; Ⓜ Tsim Sha Tsui, exit B1)

NADIR KEKLIK / SHUTTERSTOCK ©

Kowloon Mosque & Islamic Centre

Nathan Road

STREET

5 MAP P128, D2

Named after Hong Kong's only Jewish governor, Matthew Nathan, Kowloon's main drag is a bit of a traffic- and pedestrian-choked scrum of malls, jewellery stores and fashion boutiques. It's nonetheless an iconic Hong Kong scene where guesthouses rub shoulders with luxury hotels. And it's completely safe – which is just as well since you won't be able to avoid using it if you spend any time in the area. (彌敦道; Tsim Sha Tsui; M Tsim Sha Tsui, Jordan)

Kowloon Mosque & Islamic Centre

MOSQUE

6 MAP P128, D3

With its splendid dome, quartet of 11m-high minarets and lattice window tracery, the Kowloon Mosque is a captivating building and an important place of worship for the territory's 300,000-strong Islamic population. Built in 1984 (the previous mosque suffered damage during MTR construction), it can accommodate up to 3000 worshippers across three halls. The original mosque was established to serve the Indian Muslim troops of the British army who were stationed at what is now Kowloon Park.

Muslims are welcome to attend services, but non-Muslims should ask permission to enter. Remember to remove your footwear. (九龍清真寺; ☎ 852 2724 0095; 105 Nathan Rd, Tsim Sha Tsui; ⏰ 5am-10pm; Ⓜ Tsim Sha Tsui, exit C2)

Hong Kong Museum of Art

MUSEUM

7 ◉ MAP P128, D6

This excellent museum was closed at time of research while it undergoes a multimillion-dollar renovation. When open, it has galleries spread over six floors exhibiting Chinese antiquities, fine art, historical pictures and contemporary Hong Kong art. Highlights include the Xubaizhi collection of painting and calligraphy, contemporary works, and ceramics and other antiques from China. (香港藝術館; ☎ 852 2721 0116; http://hk.art.museum; 10 Salisbury Rd, Tsim Sha Tsui; adult/concession HK$10/5, Wed free; ⏰ 10am-6pm Mon-Fri, to 7pm Sat & Sun; ☻ Star Ferry, Ⓜ East Tsim Sha Tsui, exit J)

Former Marine Police Headquarters

HISTORIC BUILDING

8 ◉ MAP P128, C5

Built in 1884, this gorgeous Victorian complex is one of Hong Kong's four oldest government buildings. It was used continuously by the Hong Kong Marine Police until the 1990s, except during WWII when the Japanese navy took over. The complex is now a nakedly commercial property called 'Heritage 1881'. The original building

contains restaurants and **Hullet House**, a suite-only boutique hotel, all sitting atop high-end shopping, naturally. (前水警總部; ☎ 852 2926 8000; www.1881heritage.com; 2A Canton Rd, Tsim Sha Tsui; admission free; ⏰ 10am-10pm; ☻ Star Ferry, Ⓜ East Tsim Sha Tsui, exit L6)

Hong Kong Space Museum & Theatre

MUSEUM

9 ◉ MAP P128, D6

Updated in 2016, this golf-ball-shaped museum on the waterfront has a new permanent exhibition, 'journey of space exploration', together with high-tech 3D shows several times a day in the Stanley Ho Space Theatre. Be prepared to queue outside to get tickets for a two-hour time slot to enter the museum. (香港太空館; ☎ 852 2721 0226; www.lcsd.gov.hk; 10 Salisbury Rd, Tsim Sha Tsui; adult/concession HK$10/7, shows HK$36/16; ⏰ 1-9pm Mon & Wed-Fri, 10am-9pm Sat & Sun; ♿; Ⓜ East Tsim Sha Tsui, exit J)

Watertours

BOATING

10 ◉ MAP P128, C5

Hong Kong is perhaps best admired by boat, and this company offers a range of 'cruises' on junk-style crafts. Most worthwhile are the one-hour excursions such as the 'Symphony of Lights Tour' (HK$290), which includes unlimited free alcoholic and soft drinks. (☎ 852 2926 3868; www.watertours.com.hk; 6th fl, Carnarvon Plaza, 20 Carnarvon Rd, Tsim Sha Tsui)

Hong Kong Dolphinwatch

The **Hong Kong Dolphinwatch** (香港海豚觀察; Map p128, C5; ☎852 2984 1414; www.hkdolphinwatch.com; 15th fl, Middle Block, 1528A Star House, 3 Salisbury Rd, Tsim Sha Tsui; adult/child HK$460/230; ⊗cruises Wed, Fri & Sun) was founded in 1995 to raise awareness of Hong Kong's endangered pink dolphins. The organisation conducts dolphin-spotting cruises (three to four hours) three times weekly as long as enough people sign up. Advance booking is required. It claims that 97% of cruises sight at least one dolphin; if none are spotted, passengers are offered a free trip.

Guides assemble in the lobby of the **Kowloon Hotel** (九龍酒店; www.thekowloonhotel.com; 19-21 Nathan Rd, Tsim Sha Tsui; Ⓜ Tsim Sha Tsui, exit E) in Tsim Sha Tsui at 8.50am for the bus to Tung Chung via the Tsing Ma Bridge, from where the boat departs; the tours return in the afternoon.

It is estimated that 100 to 200 misnamed Chinese white dolphins (*Sousa chinensis*) – they are actually bubblegum pink – inhabit the coastal waters around Hong Kong, finding the brackish waters of the Pearl River estuary to be the perfect habitat. Unfortunately, these glorious mammals, which are also called Indo-Pacific humpback dolphins, are being threatened by environmental pollution and their numbers are dwindling.

Big Bus Company
BUS

 11 ◉ MAP P128, C6

If you only have a short window for sightseeing, you might consider these h op-on, hop-off, open-topped double-deckers. Three tours are available: the Kowloon Route takes in much of the Tsim Sha Tsui and Hung Hom waterfront; the Hong Kong Island Route explores Central, Admiralty, Wan Chai and Causeway Bay; and the Green Tour goes to Stanley Market and Aberdeen. (☎852 3102 9021; www.bigbustours.com; Unit KP-38, 1st fl, Star Ferry Pier, Tsim Sha Tsui; adult/child from HK$480/430; ⊗9am-6pm; ♿)

Eating

New Chettinad
SOUTH INDIAN $

 12 ✖ MAP P128, E4

Rub shoulders with Indian business people, tailors and traders at this tiny halal kitchen, the best of many in the marvellously multicultural maze that is Chungking Mansions. Perfectly crisp dosa the size of skateboards come with masala potato and dhal, or go for a multidish thali. Finish with a sweet and fiery masala ginger tea. (Shop 17, Ground fl, Chungking Mansions, 36-44 Nathan Rd, Tsim Sha Tsui; meals from HK$35; ⊗8am-11pm; Ⓜ Tsim Sha Tsui, exit N5)

GEET THEERAWAT / SHUTTERSTOCK ©

Chefs at Din Tai Fung

Yum Cha
DIM SUM $

13 MAP P128, E3

Kids will love the adorable, animal-shaped dumplings and buns at this gimmicky yet delicious dim sum eatery. Barbecue pork buns are adorned with tiny piggy faces, custard buns are anthropomorphic eggs, and bird-shaped pineapple puffs are served in little cages. Don't miss the fun takes on Canto snacks such as 'lollipop' sweet and sour chicken wings. (飲茶; 852 2751 1666; http://yumchahk.com; 3/F 20-22 Granville Rd, Tsim Sha Tsui; meals HK$100-250; 11.30am-11pm; M Tsim Sha Tsui, exit B2)

Mammy Pancake
DESSERTS $

14 MAP P128, E3

This takeaway counter serves up some of Hong Kong's best egg-ettes, those bubble-wrap waffles beloved of locals of all ages. Go plain or choose inventive flavours such as matcha, chestnut, sweet potato or pork floss. Or just pig out with a waffle sandwich oozing peanut butter and condensed milk. Expect a 15-minute wait. (媽咪雞蛋仔; 8-12 Carnarvon Rd, Tsim Sha Tsui; egg waffles HK$20-33; 11.30am-9pm Sun-Thu, to 10.30pm Fri & Sat; M Tsim Sha Tsui, exit D2)

Owls Choux Gelato   ICE CREAM $

15 ⊗ MAP P128, F4

Take a break in this cutesy dessert store where everything, from the gelato to the caramel sauce, is made in-house. Rich flavours such as pistachio, Earl Grey and black sesame can be enjoyed in a cone or sandwiched between creative choux, and smothered in sweet toppings. (32 Mody Rd, Tsim Sha Tsui; gelato from HK$38; ⊙ 3.30-10.30pm; M Tsim Sha Tsui, exit N1)

Yè Shanghai   DIM SUM $$

16 ⊗ MAP P128, B4

Dark woods and subdued lighting inspired by 1920s Shànghǎi impart an air of romance to this otherwise bustling restaurant serving exquisite Shanghainese and Zhèjiāng classics – tea-smoked duck, sweet and sour 'squirrel' fish, unctuous steamed pork belly. The only exception to this Jiāngnán harmony is the Cantonese dim sum being served at lunch, though that too is excellent. (夜上海; ☎ 852 2376 3322; www.elite-concepts.com; 6th fl, Marco Polo Hotel, Harbour City, Canton Rd, Tsim Sha Tsui; meals HK$400-800; ⊙ 11.30am-2.30pm & 6-10.30pm; M Tsim Sha Tsui, exit C2)

Din Tai Fung   SHANGHAI $$

17 ⊗ MAP P128, C4

DTF's steamers of perfectly pleated xiao long bao (Shànghǎi-style dumplings) have made this Taiwanese chain an Asia-wide institution. Order them wrapped with pork, crab, veggies or even truffle. Queues are the norm and there are no reservations, but service is excellent. Must-eats also include the fluffy steamed pork buns and the greasy-but-oh-so-good fried pork chop. (鼎泰豐; ☎ 852 2730 6928; www.dintaifung.com.hk; Shop 130, 3rd fl, Silvercord, 30 Canton Rd, Tsim Sha Tsui; meals HK$150-300; ⊙ 11.30am-10.30pm; 🚻; M Tsim Sha Tsui, exit C1)

Spring Deer   PEKING DUCK $$

18 ⊗ MAP P128, F4

Hong Kong's most authentic Northern Chinese–style roast lamb is served at this long-standing locals' favourite. Better known is the perfectly bronzed Peking duck, carved thick and served with traditional shāobǐng bread as well as the more usual steamed pancakes. Service can sometimes be as welcoming as a Běijīng winter, c 1967. Booking is essential. (鹿鳴春飯店; ☎ 852 2366 4012; 1st fl, 42 Mody Rd, Tsim Sha Tsui; meals HK$150-500; ⊙ 11.30am-3pm & 6-11pm; M East Tsim Sha Tsui, exit P3)

T'ang Court   CANTONESE, DIM SUM $$$

19 ⊗ MAP P128, C4

Deep carpets, fine silks and burgundy drapes equal a rarefied ambience at this highly praised, high-rolling Cantonese eatery with three Michelin stars inside the Langham Hotel. Tasting menus, from HK$1080 per person, are the most fuss-free way to sample the considerable kitchen skills

Tea at the Peninsula

Lording it over the southern tip of Kowloon, the throne-like **Peninsula** (c 1928; 香港半島酒店; ☎852 2920 2888; www.peninsula.com; Salisbury Rd, Tsim Sha Tsui; r/ste from HK$4000/6000; @ 🛜 ♨ ✿; MⒽTsim Sha Tsui, exit E) is one of the world's great hotels. Once called 'the finest hotel east of Suez', it now has a modern 20-storey annexe with killer harbour views, but the original building still has glorious heritage interiors. Guests sometimes arrive by landing on the rooftop helipad, or in one of the hotel's 16-strong fleet of Rolls-Royce Phantoms. But even if you can't afford that, taking afternoon tea here is a wonderful experience and a Hong Kong institution – dress neatly and be prepared to queue for a table.

on show here. (唐閣; ☎852 2375 1133; www.hongkong.langhamhotels.com; 1st fl, Langham Hotel, 8 Peking Rd, Tsim Sha Tsui; lunch/dinner from HK$700/1100; ⏱noon-2.30pm & 6-10.30pm; MⒽTsim Sha Tsui, exit L4)

Tin Lung Heen CANTONESE $$$

20 🍽 MAP P128, A1

Though the decor is imposing – Xi Jinping would feel quite at home – the service is personable and the views phenomenal at this two-Michelin star palace. The signature *char siu* (roast pork) made with Spanish Iberico pork is the priciest plate of barbecue in town, but might well be the best. (天龍軒; ☎852 2263 2270; www.ritzcarlton.com/hongkong; 102nd fl, Ritz-Carlton Hong Kong, 1 Austin Rd W, International Commerce Centre; dinner from HK$1000; ⏱noon-2.30pm & 6-10.30pm; ❄; MⒽKowloon, exit C1)

Gaddi's FRENCH $$$

21 🍽 MAP P128, D5

Collars are required for gentlemen dining at Gaddi's, a baronial French restaurant with splendid heritage interiors and a history stretching back to just after WWII. The food is traditional French (glazed duck, burgundy snails, dessert souffles), supported by a spectacular wine list. Some might find the live dinner band gratuitous, but the old-world atmosphere is palpable. (☎852 2696 6763; www.peninsula.com; 1st fl, The Peninsula, 19-21 Salisbury Rd, Tsim Sha Tsui; set lunch/dinner HK$700/2200; ⏱noon-2.30pm & 7-10.30pm; MⒽTsim Sha Tsui, exit E)

Fook Lam Moon CANTONESE, DIM SUM $$$

22 🍽 MAP P128, F2

Locals call FLM 'celebrities' canteen'. And even if you're not rich and famous, FLM will treat you as though you are. The huge menu contains expensive items such as abalone, costing at least HK$1000 per head. But it's OK to stick to the dim sum (from HK$60 a basket), which is divine and available only at lunch. (福臨門; ☏852 2366 0286; www.fooklammoon-grp.com; Shop 8, 1st fl, 53-59 Kimberley Rd, Tsim Sha Tsui; meals HK$400-2000; ⏱11.30am-2.30pm & 6-10.30pm; Ⓜ Tsim Sha Tsui, exit B1)

Drinking

InterContinental Lobby Lounge
CAFE, BAR

23 🚇 MAP P128, E6

What's that sound? No, not the chink of cup and saucer, that's your jaw hitting the marble floor as you gaze, enraptured, at Hong Kong's most fabulous harbour views through a wall of glass. It's enough to make anybody feel like a somebody, and all you have to do is order a (very expensive) drink. (☏852 2721 1211; www.hongkong-ic.intercontinental.com; Hotel InterContinental Hong Kong, 18 Salisbury Rd, Tsim Sha Tsui; ⏱7am-12.30am; 🛜; Ⓜ East Tsim Sha Tsui, exit J)

Kowloon Taproom
CRAFT BEER

24 🚇 MAP P128, D4

Plugging a crafty gap in the market between TST's hotel bars and same-same sports dives, Kowloon Taproom pours a dozen, local-only craft beers from Lion Rock, Heroes and the like, astride a fry-heavy snack list including battered 'IPA' fish and chips. The grungy, open-fronted space, its bare walls pasted with posters, is a fine people-watching perch. Beers from HK$60. (☏852 2861 0355; www.kowloon-taproom.com; 26 Ashley Rd, Tsim Sha Tsui; ⏱2pm-2am Mon-Fri, from 1pm Sat & Sun; 🛜; Ⓜ Tsim Sha Tsui, exit H)

N1 Coffee & Co
CAFE

25 🚇 MAP P128, F4

The best place to come when craving a high-quality caffeine fix in East Tsim Sha Tsui. Sandwiches and bagels are good here, too. (☏852 3568 4726; www.n1coffee.hk; 34 Mody Rd, East Tsim Sha Tsui; ⏱9am-7pm; 🛜; Ⓜ East Tsim Sha Tsui, exit N4)

Chicken HOF & Soju
BEER HALL

26 🚇 MAP P128, F1

In the middle of a Korean neighbourhood, this dark little venue hides an authentically tatty chimek (chicken and beer) bar. Korean lager starts at a wallet-friendly HK$32, and you'll need plenty of it (soju chasers optional) to wash down a hearty order of crisp fried chicken. (李家; Chicken; ☏852 2375 8080; 84 Kam Kok Mansion, Kimberley Rd, Tsim Sha Tsui; beer from HK$32; ⏱5pm-4am; Ⓜ Jordan, exit D)

Butler
COCKTAIL BAR

27 🚇 MAP P128, F4

A discreetly upscale drinking den hidden in the residential part of Tsim Sha Tsui, this Japanese bar is split over two floors, with whisky on top and cocktails beneath. Flip through whisky magazines as you watch the unfailingly polite bartenders mix up potent concoctions with precision. (🗐 852 2724 3828; 5th fl, Mody House, 30 Mody Rd, Tsim Sha Tsui; drinks around HK$200; 🕓 6.30pm-3am Tue-Sat, to 1.30am Sun; 🛜; Ⓜ East Tsim Sha Tsui, exit N2)

Vibes
LOUNGE

28 📍 MAP P128, D2

Open to the elements, this showy 5th-floor lounge bar in the Mira Hotel has greenery, water features, and exotic cabana seating (for a hefty minimum charge). Resident DJs spin downtempo electronic beats every Thursday to Saturday from 8pm. A long list of cocktails and beers is complemented by bar snacks and shisha. (🗐 852 2315 5999; www.themirahotel.com; 5th fl, Mira Hong Kong, 118 Nathan Rd, Tsim Sha Tsui; 🕓 5pm-midnight Sun-Wed, to 1am Thu-Sat; 🛜; Ⓜ Tsim Sha Tsui, exit B1)

Aqua
ROOFTOP BAR

29 📍 MAP P128, C5

Drink in harbour views from this mezzanine cocktail bar, although the best window seating is reserved for fine-dining haunt **Hutong** below. Creative cocktails (from HK$138) are reasonably priced considering you're subsidising all that panoramic glass. Fridays and Saturdays inject life into the otherwise dormant DJ booth. (🗐 852 3427 2288; www.aqua.com.hk; 29th & 30th fl, 1 Peking Rd, Tsim Sha Tsui; 🕓 4pm-2am, happy hour 4-6pm; 🛜; Ⓜ Tsim Sha Tsui, exit L5)

Felix Bar
BAR

30 📍 MAP P128, D5

Admire the views with a champagne cocktail at this Philippe Starck–designed modern European restaurant that has several distinct bar areas. (🗐 852 2315 3188; 28th fl, Peninsula Hong Kong,

Cult of Chungking

Say 'budget accommodation' and 'Hong Kong' in one breath and everyone thinks of Chungking Mansions. Built in 1961, CKM is a labyrinth of homes, guesthouses, Indian restaurants, souvenir stalls and foreign-exchange shops spread over five 17-storey blocks in the heart of Tsim Sha Tsui. According to anthropologist Gordon Mathews, it has a resident population of about 4000 and an estimated 10,000 daily visitors. More than 120 different nationalities – predominantly South Asian and African – pass through its doors in a single year.

Movie buffs note: it was Mirador Mansion, CKM's northern neighbour – and not Chungking – where Wong Kar-wai filmed most of the Hong Kong cult classic movie *Chungking Express* (1994).

Salisbury Rd, Tsim Sha Tsui; ⏱5.30pm-1.30am; 📶; Ⓜ Tsim Sha Tsui, exit E)

Shopping

K11 Select
ACCESSORIES, CLOTHING

31 🔒 MAP P128, E4

In the K11 mall, this shop – like a mini department store – is a funky destination for clothing and accessories, much of it by Hong Kong designers. **Matter Matters** employs bold colours and iconic geometric graphics on its bags and gifts. Hip multibrand store **Kapok** has menswear and unisex accessories. (Shop 101, K11 Mall, 18 Hanoi Rd, Tsim Sha Tsui; ⏱10am-10pm; Ⓜ East Tsim Sha Tsui, exit D2)

Rise Shopping Arcade
CLOTHING

32 🔒 MAP P128, F2

Bursting the seams of this minimall is cheap streetwear from Hong Kong, Korea and Japan, with a few knock-offs chucked in for good measure. Patience and a good eye could land you purchases fit for a *Vogue* photo shoot. It's best visited between 4pm and 8.30pm when most of the shops are open. (利時商場; 5-11 Granville Circuit, Tsim Sha Tsui; ⏱3-9pm; Ⓜ Tsim Sha Tsui, exit B2)

Elements
MALL

33 🔒 MAP P128, A1

Located inside the **ICC** (環球貿易廣場; www.shkp-icc.com; 1 Austin Rd W, Tsim Sha Tsui; ⏱10am-9pm),

Kowloon's most upmarket shopping mall is a confusing maze divided into five zones each themed to one of the five natural elements. As well as ample shopping and dining, it's also home to Hong Kong's largest cinema complex. (圓方; www.elementshk.com; 1 Austin Rd W, West Kowloon; ⏱11am-9pm; Ⓜ Kowloon, exit C1)

K11 Art Mall
MALL

With international clothing brands plus some edgier local offerings, K11 (see 31 🔒 Map p128, E4) is modern, compact and manageable, and also features exhibition spaces for local artists, hence its 'art mall' title. The basement is a sweet-lover's paradise, with a global array of chocolate shops. It's right above the MTR station. (18 Hanoi Rd, Tsim Sha Tsui; ⏱10am-10pm; Ⓜ East Tsim Sha Tsui, exit D2)

Harbour City
MALL

34 🔒 MAP P128, B4

A magnet for millions of tourists, this never-ending retail and dining mecca has some 700 shops arranged over four zones: kids, sport, fashion and cosmetics. You'll also find food, cafes and a cinema complex. (www.harbourcity.com.hk; 3-9 Canton Rd, Tsim Sha Tsui; ⏱10am-10pm; Ⓜ Tsim Sha Tsui, exit C1)

Worth a Trip 🔭
Chi Lin Nunnery

One of the most beautiful and arrestingly built environments in Hong Kong, this large Buddhist complex, originally dating from the 1930s, was rebuilt of wood in the style of a Tang dynasty monastery in 1998. It's serene with lotus ponds, bonsai tea plants, bougainvillea and silent nuns delivering offerings of fruit and rice to Buddha or chanting behind intricately carved screens.

志蓮淨苑

📞 852 2354 1888

www.chilin.org

5 Chi Lin Dr, Diamond Hill

admission free

🕐 nunnery 9am-4.30pm, garden 6.30am-7pm

Ⓜ Diamond Hill, exit C2

Architecture

Built to last a thousand years, Chi Lin Nunnery is the world's largest cluster of handcrafted timber buildings, exhibiting a level of artistry rarely found in other faux-ancient architecture. The design, involving interlocking sections of wood joined without a single nail, is intended to demonstrate the harmony of humans with nature.

Visiting the Nunnery

You enter through the **Sam Mun**, a series of 'three gates' representing the Buddhist precepts of compassion, wisdom and 'skilful means'. The first courtyard, which contains the delightful **Lotus Pond Garden**, gives way to the **Hall of Celestial Kings**, with a large statue of the seated Buddha surrounded by deities. Behind that is the **Main Hall**, containing a statue of the Sakyamuni Buddha.

Nan Lian Garden

Connected to the nunnery is **Nan Lian Garden**, a graceful, Tang-style park with a number of sights including a golden pagoda (pictured left), koi ponds, flower displays and ornamental rockeries. Nan Lian Garden is also the setting for Chi Lin Vegetarian and Song Cha Xie.

Nearby: Sik Sik Yuen Wong Tai Sin Temple

Just one stop away on the same MTR line, busy **Sik Sik Yuen Wong Tai Sin Temple** (嗇色園黃大仙祠; ☑852 2327 8141; www.siksikyuen.org.hk; 2 Chuk Yuen Village, Wong Tai Sin; donation HK$2; ⏰7am-5pm; Ⓜ Wong Tai Sin, exit B2) is a devout ensemble of halls, shrines, pavilions, and altars for all walks of Hong Kong society. Some come to pray, others to divine the future with *chim* – numbered bamboo 'fortune sticks' that are shaken out of a box on to the ground (they're available free from the right of the main temple). Take the noted numbers to an attendant fortune-teller to be read.

★ Top Tips

o Though an on-site tea shop sells water, it's expensive – bring your own.

o Save enough time to explore Nan Lian Garden, enjoy tea and vegetarian snacks at Chi Lin Vegetarian.

✕ Take a Break

o Don't miss eating at the nunnery's superb **Chi Lin Vegetarian** (志蓮素齋, 龍門樓; Long Men Lou; ☑852 3658 9388; 60 Fung Tak Rd, Nan Lian Garden; meals from HK$200; ⏰noon-9pm Mon-Fri, 11.30am-9pm Sat & Sun; ✓; Ⓜ Diamond Hill, exit C2) restaurant. Reserve ahead.

o For a tea break, stop at the complex's **Song Cha Xie** (松茶榭; Pavilion of Pine & Tea; ☑852 3658 9390; 60 Fung Tak Rd, Nan Lian Garden; tea from HK$160; ⏰noon-6.30pm; Ⓜ Diamond Hill, exit C2) teahouse.

o For casual eats, try the food court at Hollywood Plaza, the shopping mall above the Diamond Hill MTR station.

Explore ◈
Yau Ma Tei
& Mong Kok

Indigenous Yau Ma Tei is old Hong Kong at its most captivating. Soak up the lingering vibes of yesteryear Hong Kong in its mosaic of neon, night markets, guesthouses and martial-arts dens, or explore the sardine-packed commercialism of Mong Kok and its shops that sell everything from electronics to clothing and sporting goods.

The Short List

◦ **Mido Cafe (p152)** *Breakfasting at Kowloon's most famous tea cafe*

◦ **Yue Hwa Chinese Products Emporium (p154)** *Stocking up on quirky gifts and souvenirs*

◦ **Temple Street Night Market (p144)** *Soaking up the intoxicating mix of commerce, culture and street food at Hong Kong's liveliest night market*

◦ **Canton Singing House (p154)** *Enjoying a festive night out with the locals at one of Yau Ma Tei's old-fashioned singalong parlours*

◦ **Shanghai Street (p150)** *Shopping for woks, cleavers and tree-trunk carving boards in old-timey Hong Kong*

Getting There & Around

Ⓜ Jordan, Yau Ma Tei and Mong Kok stations are on the Tsuen Wan line.

🚌 2, 6, 6A and 9 go up and down Nathan Rd between Tsim Sha Tsui and Yau Ma Tei.

Neighbourhood Map on p148

Top Sight

Temple Street Night Market

When night falls and neon buzzes, Hong Kong's liveliest market rattles into life. Temple St extends southwards from Man Ming Lane to Nanking St, cut in two by the historic Tin Hau Temple (p147). It's great for the bustling atmosphere, dai pai dong (food stalls), free Cantonese opera performances and fortune-telling. The market is liveliest between 7pm and 10pm.

⊙ MAP P148, D6

廟街夜市

Temple St, Yau Ma Tei

⊙ 6-11pm

Ⓜ Yau Ma Tei, exit C

A Century of Commerce

Back at the turn of the 20th century, snack and trinket vendors would gather around Tin Hau Temple (p147), the social and spiritual heart of Yau Ma Tei, to hawk their wares to temple-goers. By the 1920s, this commerce had grown into a regular market as vendors would set up further and further from the temple itself. It wasn't until the 1980s, however, that 'Thieves Market', as it was then known, started to appear in the tourist guidebooks.

Eating Out

For alfresco dining, head for Woo Sung St, running parallel to the east, or to the section of Temple St north of the temple. You can get anything from a bowl of wonton noodles to oyster omelettes and Nepalese curries. There are also seafood and hotpot restaurants in the area. For an unusual experience, take a seat at a singalong parlour and order delivery.

Seeing the Future

Every evening a gaggle of fortune-tellers sets up tents in the middle of the market, where they make predictions about your life (from HK$100) by reading your face and palm, or based on your date of birth. Some keep birds that have been trained to pick out 'fortune' cards. Most operators speak some English.

Alfresco Opera

If you're in luck, you'll catch snippets of a Cantonese opera performed under the stars. Some of the most famous stars of the opera stage began their careers in this humble fashion – or so they say.

★ Top Tips

○ While the majority of sellers have no price tags on their goods, some do. Use those to gain an idea of what a semi-reasonable price might be before bargaining at tag-less stalls.

○ Touts will try to hustle you to their seafood stalls – no need to resist, as they're pretty much all the same.

✕ Take a Break

Upgrade your street-stall experience by checking out the hip and stylish food court beneath **Eaton Hotel** (香港逸東酒店; ☎ 852 2782 1818; www.hongkong. eatonhotels.com; 380 Nathan Rd, Yau Ma Tei; r HK$2350-3200, ste from HK$3250; @ 🛜 🏊; Ⓜ Jordan, exit B1) a couple of blocks away.

Snag a prebedtime snack of milk tea and egg toast at Australia Dairy Company (p152).

Walking Tour 🥾

Kowloon's Teeming Market Streets

Peel yourself away from the glitzy gauntlet of commerce around Tsim Sha Tsui and market life takes over in Kowloon. This northern walk around Yau Ma Tei and Mong Kok weaves through streets where all life congregates.

Walk Facts

Start Prince Edward MTR station, exit A

End Jordan MTR station, exit A

Length 4.5km; two hours

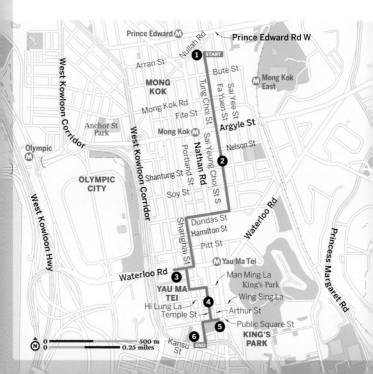

❶ Goldfish Market

A 10-minute walk east from Prince Edward station (exit A) will get you to **Flower Market Road**, lined with fragrant and exotic blooms. Double back and start heading south on Tung Choi St. Walk two blocks to the **Goldfish Market**, a dozen or so shops trading in these extravagantly hued fish. You'll see an amazing variety, with the real rarities commanding high prices.

❷ Ladies' Market

Now sharpen your elbows! Tung Choi St market, also known as the **Ladies' Market** (通菜街, 女人街; www.ladies-market.hk; ⏰noon-11.30pm), is crammed with shoppers and stalls selling mostly inexpensive clothing and trinkets. Vendors start setting up their stalls as early as noon, but it's best to get here between 1pm and 6pm when there's much more on offer.

❸ Fruit Market

Head west along Waterloo Rd and you'll pass by the art deco-styled **Yau Ma Tei Theatre** (油麻地戲院; www.lcsd.gov.hk/ymtt; ⏰box office 1-8pm), popular for Cantonese opera, before reaching historic **Yau Ma Tei Wholesale Fruit Market** (油麻地果欄; ⏰24hr). Founded in 1913, it still has pre-WWII signboards above the stalls. In the '80s the market was a hotbed of triad gang activity. The main wholesale action happens after dark (especially just before dawn), but it's also a retail market by day, so you can visit for freshly cut durian.

❹ Temple Street Night Market

Go south on Reclamation St, turning left on to Man Ming Lane until you hit the top of Temple St. Here, beneath naked light bulbs, hundreds of stalls at the Temple Street Night Market (p144) sell a vast array of booty from sex toys to luggage. The market runs right down to Jordan Rd; consider ducking into one of the Cantonese singing parlours (p154) along the street for a hyperlocal karaoke-type experience.

❺ Tin Hau Temple

Fragrant smoke curls from incense spirals at **Tin Hau Temple** (天后廟; www.ctc.org.hk; ⏰8am-5pm); it was here that the market started in the 1920s, as hawkers congregated to sell food and trinkets to worshippers. You might still see fortune-tellers nearby, using everything from tarot cards to palmistry and even tame sparrows to deliver their predictions.

❻ Jade Market

A good place to pick up an inexpensive gift (though avoid actual jade unless you know your stuff), the large covered **Jade Market** (玉器市場; ⏰10am-6pm) contains dozens of stalls selling jade of all grades as well as pretty, vintage-y ceramic-bead necklaces and bracelets, and coloured wooden beads with double happiness signs. At Jordan Rd turn east, then south into Nathan Rd to find Jordan MTR station.

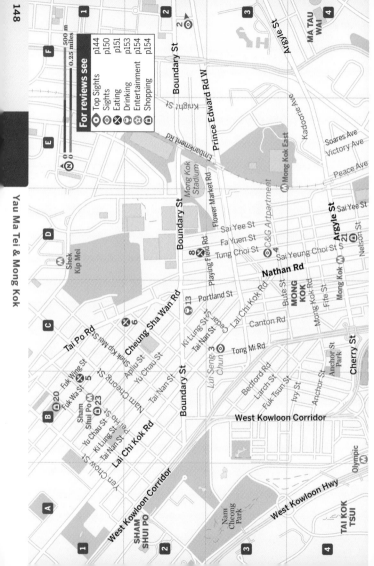

Yau Ma Tei & Mong Kok

500 m
0.25 miles

SHAM
SHUI PO

TAI KOK
TSUI

West Kowloon Corridor

West Kowloon Hwy

Nam
Cheong Park

West Kowloon Corridor

MONG
KOK

MA TAU
WAI

Boundary St

Prince Edward Rd W

Mong Kok
Stadium

Mong Kok East

Argyle St

Nathan Rd

Cherry St

Tai Po Rd

Cheung Sha Wan Rd

Boundary St

Shek
Kip Mei

Yen Chow St
Fuk Wing St
Fuk Wa St
Sham
Shui Po
Yu Chau St
Ki Lung St
Tai Nan St
Lai Chi Kok Rd

Nam Cheong St
Apliu St
Yu Chau St
Shek Kip Mei St

Ki Lung St
Tai Nan St
Boundary St

Lui Seng
Chun

Portland St
Tong Mi Rd
Canton Rd
Lai Chi Kok St
Cedar St

Bedford Rd
Larch St
Fuk Tsun St
Ivy St
Anchor St
Anchor St
Anchor
Park

Bute St
Fife St
Mong Kok Rd
Mong Kok Rd
Nelson St

Sai Yee St
Fa Yuen St
Tung Choi St
Sai Yeung Choi St S

Playing Field Rd
Flower Market Rd
Embankment Rd

Kadoorie Ave
Soares Ave
Victory Ave
Peace Ave

Knight St

Argyle St
Sai Yee St

Olympic

20
23
5
6
8
13
2
21
4
3

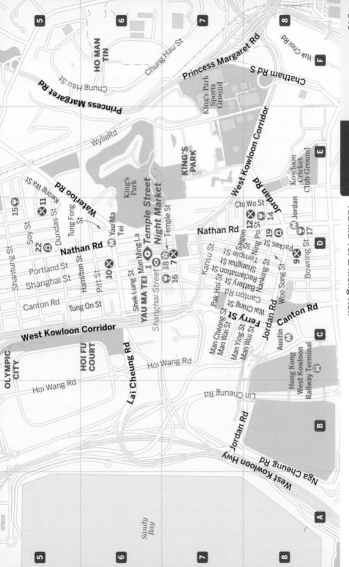

Sights

Shanghai Street   STREET

1 ⊙ MAP P148, D6

Strolling down Shanghai St will return you to a time long past. Once Kowloon's main drag, it's flanked by stores selling Chinese wedding gowns, sandalwood incense and Buddha statues, plus mahjong parlours and an old pawn shop (at the junction with Saigon St). This is a terrific place for souvenirs – fun picks include wooden moon-cake moulds stamped with images of fish, pigs or lucky sayings, bamboo steamer baskets, long chopsticks meant for stirring pots and pretty ceramic bowls. (上海街; Yau Ma Tei; Ⓜ Yau Ma Tei, exit C)

Kowloon Walled City Park   PARK

2 ⊙ MAP P148, F2

Try to imagine that this 1.2-hectare ornamental park, built by the British in the early 1990s, was just a few years earlier one of the most infamous residential estates the world had ever seen. Completely unplanned, it was home to a claustrophobic press of 40,000 Chinese people living in teetering shanty towers 15 storeys high, connected by a network of narrow passageways and staircases that never saw daylight, hence its Cantonese nickname, 'City of Darkness'.

Kowloon Walled City was also infested with gangs, brothels and opium dens, and neither government wanted anything to do with it. The British eventually relocated all the residents, tore it down and put this park in its place, which harkens back to the original Chinese military fort that was built here in 1847. The fort remained a Chinese-run enclave throughout British rule, which partly explains its unregulated rise into Kowloon Walled City. Surprisingly, traces of the original fort, including cannon and the partly rebuilt almshouse, remain (it now houses a small history exhibit on the Walled City).

You can also see exhumed sections of the original south gate and sign. A scale model of the Walled City by the park's entrance gives an indication of its staggering density. Confusingly, Kowloon Walled City Park is effectively inside the larger and more prosaic Carpenter Road Park, delineated, appropriately, by an encircling stone wall. (九龍寨城公園; 📞852 2716 9962; www.lcsd. gov.hk; Tung Tau Tsuen, Tung Tsing, cnr Carpenter & Junction Rds, Kowloon City; ⏰park 6.30am-11pm, exhibition 10am-6pm Thu-Tue; Ⓜ Lok Fu, exit B)

Lui Seng Chun   HISTORIC BUILDING

3 ⊙ MAP P148, C3

Hugging a street corner is this beautiful four-storey Chinese 'shophouse' belonging to a school of Chinese medicine. Constructed circa 1931, it features a mix of Chinese and European architectural styles – verandahs, urn-shaped balustrades and other fanciful takes on a neoclassical Italian villa. The well-preserved ground floor, which has a herbal tea shop, is open to the public. Free guided tours (45 minutes) to the upper-floor clinics are available by registration. They're in Cantonese, but exhibits have bilingual labels. (雷春生堂; ☎852 3411 0628; http://scm.hkbu.edu.hk/lsctour; 119 Lai Chi Kok Rd, cnr Tong Mi Rd, Mong Kok; admission free; ⏰guided tour 2.30pm & 4pm Mon-Fri, 9.30am & 11am Sat, consultation 9am-1pm & 2-8pm Mon-Sat, 9am-1pm Sun; Ⓜ Prince Edward, exit C2)

C&G Artpartment GALLERY

4 ◉ MAP P148, D3

Clara and Gum, the founders of this edgy art space up three flights of stairs in a residential building, are passionate about nurturing the local art scene and representing socially minded artists. C&G also runs art courses. See the website for details and current exhibitions.

(☎852 2390 9332; www.candg-artpartment.com; 3rd fl, 222 Sai Yeung Choi St S, Mong Kok; ⏰2-7.30pm Thu, Fri, Sun & Mon, from 11am Sat; Ⓜ Prince Edward, exit B2)

Eating

Kung Wo Tofu Factory TOFU $

5 ✖ MAP P148, B1

Regulars come to this charming 50-year-old shop for fresh soy milk, pan-fried tofu and sweet tofu pudding (HK$12), made the traditional way from beans ground with a hand-operated millstone. The silky tofu has nutty notes, and the hue is off-white – reassuringly imperfect, just like the service. (公和荳品廠; ☎852 2386 6871; 118 Pei Ho St, Sham Shui Po; dishes HK$8-30; ⏰9am-9pm; Ⓜ Sham Shui Po, exit B2)

Kowloon Walled City Park

Taoist Temples

If you see temples guarded by fierce-looking gods, they are likely to be Taoist. Taoism is an indigenous religion that originated in the shamanistic roots of Chinese civilisation. Unlike evangelical religions stressing crusading and conversion, Taoism addresses practical needs such as cures for illnesses, protection from evil spirits and funerary requirements. In the first two weeks of the Lunar New Year, millions in Hong Kong pay their respects at Taoist temples, such as Sik Sik Yuen Wong Tai Sin (p141).

Tim Ho Wan   DIM SUM $

6 🍴 MAP P148, C2

Renowned as the first budget dim sum eatery to receive a Michelin star way back in 2010, Tim Ho Wan has spread from its Mong Kok roots (opened by a former Four Seasons dim sum chef) into a miniempire, with five restaurants in Hong Kong (this is the second branch, the original closed) and global franchises everywhere from Sydney to Singapore. (添好運點心專門店; 𝄡852 2788 1226; www.timhowan.com.hk; 9-11 Fuk Wing St, Sham Shui Po; dim sum from HK$28; ⏰10am-9.30pm, from 9am Sat & Sun; Ⓜ Sham Shui Po, exit B1)

Mido Café   CAFE $

7 🍴 MAP P148, D7

Kowloon's most famous tea cafe, this highly instagrammable *cha chaan tang* (teahouse; c 1950) with mosaic tiles and metal lattice-work stands astride a street corner that comes to life at sundown. Go upstairs and take a seat next to a wall of iron-framed windows overlooking Tin Hau Temple (p147). (美都餐室; 𝄡852 2384 6402; 63 Temple St, Yau Ma Tei; meals HK$40-90; ⏰9am-10pm; Ⓜ Yau Ma Tei, exit B2)

One Dim Sum   DIM SUM $

8 🍴 MAP P148, D2

This cheery little place is known for all-day, bang-for-the-buck dim sum. Tick your selections on the menu card; the quality is more than a match for Tim Ho Wan nearby. One Dim Sum didn't retain the Michelin star it bagged in 2012, but it did keep the crowds. That said, the wait is usually under 30 minutes. (一點心; 𝄡852 2789 2280; Shop 1 & 2, Kenwood Mansion, 15 Playing Field Rd, Mong Kok; meals HK$40-100; ⏰10.30am-midnight, from 9.30am Sat & Sun; Ⓜ Prince Edward, exit A)

Australia Dairy Company   CAFE $

9 🍴 MAP P148, D8

Long waits and hurried service are the standard at this beloved Hong Kong *cha chaan tang*, famed for its steamed milk or egg puddings (HK$30), which are best gobbled up ice-cold. Locals breakfast here on scrambled-egg sandwiches and macaroni in a soup with ham. An experience to be had, for sure, but not a relaxing one! (澳洲牛奶公司; ☎852 2730 1356; 47-49 Parkes St, Jordan; meals HK$30-50; ⏱7.30am-11pm Wed-Mon; Ⓜ Jordan, exit C2)

Sun Sin
NOODLES $

10 ✚ MAP P148, D6

A stylish brisket shop in a 'hood known for brothels, Sun Sin serves succulent cuts of beef in a broth with radish, in a tomato soup or as a curry. If you just fancy a snack, you can get a ladle of chunky brisket dolloped inside a hollowed-out bread roll. (新仙清湯腩; ☎852 2332 6872; 37 Portland St, Yau Ma Tei; meals HK$40-65; ⏱11am-midnight; Ⓜ Yau Ma Tei, exit B2)

Good Hope Noodle
NOODLES $

11 ✚ MAP P148, D5

This 40-year-old shop has retained its Michelin commendation and fan following. Now the al dente egg noodles, bite-sized wontons and silky congee that have won hearts for decades continue to be cooked the old way, but are served in neat, modern surrounds. (好旺角麵家; ☎852 2384 6898; Shop 5-6, 18 Fa Yuen St, Mong Kok; meals HK$30-90; ⏱11am-12.45am; Ⓜ Mong Kok, exit D3)

Nathan Congee & Noodle
NOODLES $

12 ✚ MAP P148, D8

This humble shop has been serving up tasty Canto fare for the past half-century. Order a side of fritters to dunk in your congee, tackle a pyramidal rice dumpling, or conquer the blanched fish skin tossed with parsley and peanuts. (彌敦粥麵家; ☎852 2771 4285; 11 Saigon St, Yau Ma Tei; meals HK$60; ⏱7.30am-11.30pm; Ⓜ Jordan, exit B2)

Drinking

Bound
BAR

13 🍷 MAP P148, C2

You could squish a dozen Hong Kong bars together and they still wouldn't have as much personality as this boho hang-out with its art-adorned walls, flashes of pink neon, indie playlist and craft-beer fridge. Bound could almost be the HQ of a hip marketing agency, but don't be put off – staff are really nice, and the coffee is fabulous. (32 Boundary St, Prince Edward; ⏱11am-2am; 🛜; Ⓜ Prince Edward, exit D)

Horizonte Lounge
ROOFTOP BAR

14 🍷 MAP P148, D8

You'll feel like Rapunzel atop her tower at this lofty perch in the Kowloon skyline. From all four (low) walls, panoramic vistas reveal the great mass of urban jungle-meets-island paradise in all its chaotic glory. Order a drink at the counter below then take your seat outside for sunset. Don't look down. (☎852 2121 9888; www.hotelmadera.com.hk; Madera Hotel, 1-9 Cheong Lok St, Yau Ma Tei; ⏱5pm-1am; 🛜; Ⓜ Jordan, exit B1)

TAP: The Ale Project   CRAFT BEER

15 🍴 MAP P148, D5

On a lively strip of independent eateries and bars, Tap pours around 20 local craft ales in its exposed brick, blue-painted space. Staff aren't the friendliest, but they will let you taste before you buy. You'll love the excellent sandwiches, from sourdough grilled cheese to grander fusion assemblages, some of which can be bought by half. (📞852 2468 2010; 15 Hak Po St, Mong Kok; ⏰noon-1am; 🛜; Ⓜ Mong Kok, exit E2)

Kubrick Bookshop Café   CAFE

16 🍴 MAP P148, D7

An eclectic, student-y crowd packs out this bookshop-cafe attached to the **Broadway Cinematheque** (百老匯電影中心). Pop in for a coffee and browse through a collection of art, film and cultural-studies titles. You can also chow on a burger or pasta bowl. (📞852 2384 8929; www.kubrick.com.hk; Shop H2, Prosperous Garden, 3 Public Sq St, Yau Ma Tei; ⏰11.30am-9.30pm; 🛜; Ⓜ Yau Ma Tei, exit C)

Boo   BAR, KARAOKE

17 🍴 MAP P148, D8

This low-key gay bar overlooking Nathan Rd pours good-value cocktails (HK$78). It's a friendly, easygoing place to hang out, though the blare of karaoke isn't conducive to a quiet drink. A DJ spins on Saturdays after 7pm. (📞852 2736 6168; 5th fl, Pearl Oriental Tower, 225 Nathan Rd, Jordan; ⏰7pm-2am Sun-Thu, to 4am Fri, 9pm-4am Sat, happy hour 7-9pm; Ⓜ Jordan, exit C1)

Entertainment

Canton Singing House   LIVE MUSIC

18 ⭐ MAP P148, D7

The oldest and most atmospheric of Temple St's singalong parlours, Canton resembles a film set with mirror balls and glowing shrines. Singers take to the stage one after another to belt out the oldies; some customers applaud between glugs of beer, others are too busy with card games. Every character in here looks like they have a story to tell. (艷陽天; 49-51 Temple St, Yau Ma Tei; HK$20; ⏰3-7pm & 8pm-5am; Ⓜ Yau Ma Tei, exit C)

Shopping

Yue Hwa Chinese Products Emporium   DEPARTMENT STORE

19 🔒 MAP P148, D8

This five-storey behemoth is one of few old-school Chinese department stores left in the city. Products include silk scarves, traditional Chinese baby clothes and embroidered slippers, cheap and expensive jewellery, pretty patterned chopsticks and ceramics, plastic acupuncture models and calligraphy equipment. The top floor is all about tea, with vendors offering free sips. Food is in the basement. (裕華國貨; 📞852 3511 2222; www.yuehwa.com; 301-309

Mahjong Parlours

In the 1950s, the four-player game of mahjong was so popular that the British, despite their antigambling policy, began issuing licences to mahjong parlours. Brightly lit and filled with cigarette smoke, parlours were often featured in gangster films as they were associated with the triads – the Hong Kong Mafia.

Now with the police keeping a close eye on things, the few remaining parlours on Shanghai St are are little more than the noisy playgrounds of hardcore players. Most have signs reading '麻將娛樂' ('mahjong entertainment') and you can enter for a peek, but picture-taking is forbidden.

Nathan Rd, Jordan; ⏰10am-10pm; Ⓜ Jordan, exit A)

Golden Computer Arcade & Golden Shopping Center ELECTRONICS

20 🔒 MAP P148, B1

Occupying three floors of a building just across from Sham Shui Po MTR station, Golden Computer Arcade is where the techies go for their low-cost computers and peripherals. The 3Cs are generally considered the best shops – **Centralfield**, **Capital** and **Comdex**. (黃金電腦商場、高登電腦中心; www.goldenarcade.org; 146-152 Fuk Wa St, Sham Shui Po; ⏰11am-9pm; Ⓜ Sham Shui Po, exit D2)

Showa Film & Camera VINTAGE

21 🔒 MAP P148, D4

Shutterbugs and vintage shoppers will love this boho store hawking retro film cameras, lenses, accessories and gifts. Staff are passionate and chatty, and they also have a first-rate film-developing service. (☎852 6541 5621; www.showa-store.com; 3rd fl, 66 Sai Yeung Choi St, Mong Kok; ⏰2-9pm; Ⓜ Mong Kok, exit D3)

Sino Centre MALL

22 🔒 MAP P148, D5

The go-to place for all things related to Asian comics and anime, the tiny stores in this mall sell everything from kidult figurines to vintage Casio watches and video games. (信和中心; 582-592 Nathan Rd, Mong Kok; ⏰10am-10pm; Ⓜ Yau Ma Tei, exit A2)

Apliu Street Flea Market MARKET

23 🔒 MAP P148, B1

A geek's heaven, this grungy flea market specialises in all things digital and electronic. The market spills over into Pei Ho St. (鴨寮街; Apliu St, btwn Nam Cheong & Yen Chow Sts, Sham Shui Po; ⏰noon-midnight; Ⓜ Sham Shui Po, exit A1)

Worth a Trip 👀
Ping Shan Heritage Trail

This meandering 1km trail through three old but lively villages in the northwestern New Territories features 12 thoughtfully restored historic buildings and a museum at Ping Shan dedicated to the powerful Tang clan, the founders of the spectacular 500-year-old Ping Shan Village. The Tangs are believed to be some of Hong Kong's earliest immigrants.

屏山文物徑

📞 852 2617 1959

Hang Tau Tsuen, Ping Shan, Yuen Long

🕙 ancestral halls & Tsui Sing Lau Pagoda 9am-1pm & 2-5pm, closed Tue

Ⓜ Tin Shui Wai, exit E

Tang Clan Gallery

Start with the **Ping Shan Tang Clan Gallery** (屏山鄧族文物館; ☎852 2617 1959; Hang Tau Tsuen, Ping Shan, Yuen Long; admission free; ⊙10am-5pm Tue-Sun; ᕒPing Shan) at the eastern end of the trail. Housed in a former police station, the gallery showcases the history of the Tangs. The colourful collections include a traditional sedan chair, ritual wares and a giant wooden bed. The building itself was constructed in 1899 and was a colonial outpost to monitor 'untoward' villagers.

Temple, Chamber & Study Hall

Leaving the Tang Clan Gallery, retrace your steps to Ping Ha Rd and turn right. The small **Hung Shing Temple** is on your right-hand side, followed by **Ching Shu Hin Chamber** and **Kun Ting Study Hall** (pictured left) when you turn right again.

Two Large Ancestral Halls

North of Hung Shing Temple, Shu Hin Chamber and Kun Ting Study Hall are the **Tang Clan Ancestral Hall** (鄧氏宗祠; Hang Tau Tsuen, Ping Shan, Yuen Long; admission free; ⊙9am-1pm & 2-5pm, closed Tue; ⋈Tin Shui Wai, exit E) and **Yu Kiu Ancestral Hall**, two of Hong Kong's largest ancestral halls. The Tangs justifiably brag about them, especially the one that bears their name, as it follows a three-halls-two-courtyards structure indicative of the clan's prestigious status in the imperial court.

Tsui Sing Lau Pagoda

There are some more temples and an old well ahead. At the end of the heritage trail is small, three-storey **Tsui Sing Lau Pagoda** (聚星樓; Ping Ha Rd, Ping Shan Heritage Trail; admission free; ⊙9am-1pm & 2-5pm, closed Tue; ᕒTin Shui Wai), the only surviving ancient pagoda in Hong Kong.

★ Top Tips

○ Tsui Sing Lau Pagoda is closest to the MTR station, but do not start there unless you already know about the history of the village.

○ The view from the verandah of the Ping Shan Tang Clan Gallery is nice.

✖ Take a Break

Mrs Tang Cafe (華嫂冰室; ☎852 2617 2232; Hang Tau Tsuen, Ping Shan, Yuen Long; meals from HK$23; ⊙8am-1pm & 2-5pm Mon-Sat) offers satisfying *cha chaan tang* (teahouse) fare but closes for lunch.

Accro Coffee (☎852 9430 1433; Shop 8, Ground fl, Fook Cheong Bldg, 21-27 Ma Wang Rd, Yuen Long; ⊙noon-midnight; ⋈Long Ping, exit B1) makes seriously good coffee.

Worth a Trip 🔭
Sai Kung Peninsula

Sai Kung Peninsula is one of the last havens left in Hong Kong for hikers, swimmers and boaters, and most of it is part of the stunning Hong Kong Global Geopark. Small ferries depart from the waterfront at Sai Kung Town for nearby island beaches, a journey to any of which is rewarding. Moored boats sell seafood to customers on the pier. The atmosphere is unbeatable.

西貢半島
🚌 92, Ⓜ Choi Hung,
minibus 1A, 1M, 🚌 299X,
Ⓜ Sha Tin East Rail

Hong Kong Global Geopark

The breathtaking, Unesco-listed **Hong Kong Global Geopark** (香港地質公園; www.geopark.gov.hk) spans 50 sq km and comprises two regions of spectacular rock formations – volcanic (140 million years old) and sedimentary (400 million years old). The best way to experience either region is by guided boat tour (about HK$300). The Volcano Discovery Centre (www.volcanodiscoverycentre.hk) has details. Tours to the sedimentary rock region also take in old villages such as 400-year-old Lai Chi Wo.

High Island Reservoir Dam

High Island Reservoir East Dam (萬宜水庫東壩; www.ecotoursaikung.com) is the most easily accessible part of Hong Kong Global Geopark and the only place where you can touch the hexagonal rock columns. The scenery is surreal and made even more so by the presence of thousands of dolosse blocks (huge cement barriers shaped like jacks) placed along the coast to break sea waves.

Island-Hopping

Several islands encircle the peninsula and boat trips are a delightful way to see Sai Kung. **Pak Sha Chau** and **Kiu Tsui Chau** have popular beaches. The charming 0.24-sq-km 'Catholic' island of **Yim Tin Tsai** has a chapel and its own heritage trail. **Kau Sai Chau** is home to a golf course and 19th-century temple. Boats leave from the piers on the waterfront at Sai Kung Town.

Tai Long Wan Trail

The northern end of Sai Kung Peninsula has several wonderful hikes, including the breathtaking 12km Tai Long Wan Hiking Trail. It starts from the end of Sai Wan Rd and passes through beautiful coves including Sai Wan, Tai Long Wan and Chek Keng. On weekdays you're likely to have the trail to yourself. The walk takes five to six hours.

★ Top Tips

○ Near the Sai Kung town pier, you'll find one of the liveliest fish markets in Hong Kong, where fishermen sell their catch directly from their boats.

○ Hiring a private boat from Sai Kung Waterfront Promenade to the geopark is possible, but it's more expensive than taking a tour and they don't come with a guide: book tours early.

○ To gain another perspective, explore the geopark by kayak and snorkel with a guided tour from **Kayak and Hike** (☑ 852 9300 5197; www.kayak-and-hike.com).

✕ Take a Break

Sai Kung Town boasts excellent Chinese seafood restaurants, especially along the attractive waterfront. Try Michelin-starred **Loaf On** (六福菜館; ☑ 852 2792 9966; 49 See Cheung St, Sai Kung; dishes from HK$150; ⏰ 11am-10pm; 🚌 1); reservations recommended).

Explore

Trip to Macau

Macau may be known as the Vegas of the East, but the city has so much more to offer than casinos. It's where fortresses, cathedrals and streets evoking the style of its former Portuguese masters, mingle with Chinese temples and shrines. And, of course, no trip to Macau is complete without Macanese food, a delicious celebration of hybridism.

The Short List

○ **Ruins of the Church of St Paul (p162)** *Admiring then trying to take a photo, sans crowd, of this 17th-century facade*

○ **Clube Militar de Macau (p172)** *Enjoying delicious Portuguese fare in a distinguished colonial building*

○ **Church of St Joseph (p168)** *Peering at the facade and the interiors of Macau's most beautiful church*

○ **Eight (p173)** *Savouring a lavish meal at this award-winning gourmet restaurant*

○ **Guia Fortress & Chapel (p169)** *Taking in panoramic views of the city*

Getting There & Around

⚓ Most travellers arrive in Macau by ferry from Hong Kong. If you are coming from mainland China, you can take the ferry or a bus from Guǎngdōng.

✈ Macau International Airport is connected to a number of destinations in Asia, including mainland China. If you are coming from outside Asia, fly to Hong Kong and take a ferry to Macau without going through Hong Kong customs.

Neighbourhood Map on p166

Grand Lisboa (p169) SEAN HSU / SHUTTERSTOCK ©

Top Sight 📷

Ruins of the Church of St Paul

The most treasured icon in Macau, the towering facade and stairway are all that remain of this early-17th-century Jesuit church. With its statues, portals and engravings that effectively make up a 'sermon in stone' and a Biblia pauperum (Bible of the poor), the church was one of the greatest monuments to Christianity in Asia.

◉ MAP P166, C3

大三巴牌坊, Ruinas de Igreja de São Paulo

Calçada de São Paulo

admission free

🚌 8A, 17, 26, disembark at Luís de Camões Garden

Colonial History

The church was designed by an Italian Jesuit and built in 1602 by Japanese Christian exiles and Chinese craftsmen. After the expulsion of the Jesuits, a military battalion was stationed here. In 1835 a fire erupted in the kitchen of the barracks, destroying everything, except what you see today.

Facade

The facade (pictured left) has five tiers. At the top is a dove, representing the Holy Spirit, surrounded by stone carvings of the sun, moon and stars. Beneath that is a statue of the infant Jesus accompanied by the implements of the Crucifixion. In the centre of the third tier stands the Virgin Mary being assumed bodily into heaven along with angels and two flowers: the peony, representing China, and the chrysanthemum, representing Japan. Just below the pediment, on the right side of the facade, is a dragon surmounted by the Holy Virgin. To the right of the Virgin is a carving of the tree of life and the apocalyptic woman (Mary) slaying a seven-headed hydra; the Japanese kanji next to her reads: 'The holy mother tramples the heads of the dragon'.

The facade is approached by six flights of 11 stairs each, with an attractive balustrade running up each side.

Museum

The small **Museum of Sacred Art & Crypt** (天主教藝術博物館和墓室, Museu de Arte Sacra e Cripta; Calçada de São Paulo; admission free; ⊘9am-6pm Wed-Mon, to 2pm Tue; 🚌8A, 17, 26, disembark at Luís de Camões Garden) contains carved wooden statues, silver chalices and oil paintings, as well as the remains of Vietnamese and Japanese Christians martyred in the 17th century.

★ Top Tips

o If you want to take pictures of the ruins without the crowds, go before 9am or after 6pm.

o To the southwest of the ruins lies Travessa da Paixao, aka Lover's Lane, where you'll find a row of handsome old buildings.

o Don't miss the nearby St Lazarus Church District (p168), which is much less crowded than the St Paul area but features some of the city's most beautiful architecture.

✕ Take a Break

o Have a cocktail and possibly catch some music at nearby Macau Soul (p174).

o Savour an elegant meal at **Albergue 1601** (✆853 2836 1601; www.albergue1601.com; 8 Calçada da Igreja de São Lazaro; meals MOP$300-600; ⊘noon-3pm & 6-10.30pm Mon-Fri, noon-10.30pm Sat & Sun; ❄; 🚌7, 8), a colonial courtyard building in the St Lazarus Church District.

Walking Tour 🥾

Exploring Taipa & Coloane Islands

South of Macau Peninsula, the former islands of Taipa and Coloane are joined together by a strip of reclaimed land named Cotai that houses Macau's megacasinos. Taipa has lovely Macanese houses and quaint boutiques, while Coloane is a laid-back village with shipyards and beaches. The latter was once a haven for pirates but today largely retains Macau's old way of life.

Walk Facts

Start Taipa Village; take bus 22 or 33 from the peninsula

End Coloane

Length 6km; two hours

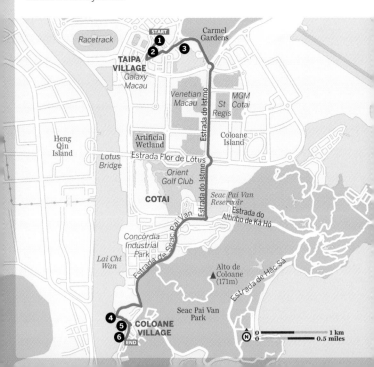

❶ Taipa Village

The historical part of Taipa is best preserved in this **village** (氹仔舊城區; 🚌 22, 26, 33) in the south of the island. With a tidy sprawl of traditional Chinese shops and some excellent restaurants, it is punctuated by grand colonial villas, churches and ancient temples. Its heart lies between Rua do Regedor, Rua Correia da Silva and Rua do Delegado.

❷ Pak Tai Temple

Pak Tai Temple (北帝廟; Largo Camões, Rua do Regedor; ⏱ 8.30am-5pm) sits quietly in a breezy square framed by old trees. It is dedicated to a martial deity – the Taoist God (*Tai*) of the North (*Pak*) – who defeated the Demon King who was terrorising the universe. A pair of Chinese lions guards the entrance to the temple. On the third day of the third lunar month, Cantonese opera performances take place here.

❸ Taipa Houses-Museum

Further afield, the pastel-toned **villas** (龍環葡韻住宅式博物館, Casa Museum da Taipa; 📞 853 2882 7103; Avenida da Praia, Carmo Zone; admission free; ⏱ 10am-6.30pm Tue-Sun; 👫; 🚌 11, 15, 22, 28A, 30, 33, 34) here were once the summer residences of middle-class Macanese; now they're museums showcasing Portuguese traditions and local life in the early 20th century.

❹ Coloane's Stilt Houses

Head to Coloane by bus 21A and alight at its urban centre – the old **fishing village** (路環村). In **Rua Dos Navegantes**, there are a few stilt houses of colourful corrugated metal, that were once landing spots for houseboats. You'll see them near **Largo do Cais**, the square just off the old pier of Coloane. From the square, take the slope to the right of the Servicos de Alfangega building. After two minutes, you'll see the cavernous cadaver of a shipyard, also on stilts.

❺ Chapel of St Francis Xavier

One of Coloane's highlights is this eccentric **chapel** (聖方濟各教堂, Capela de São Francisco Xavier; Rua do Caetano, Largo Eduardo Marques, Coloane; ⏱ 9.30am-5.30pm), built in 1928, which contains paintings of the infant Christ with a Chinese Madonna and other artefacts that illustrate how Christianity and colonialism were intertwined.

❻ Chinese-Portuguese Fare & Egg Tarts

Finish your walk with a Chinese-Portuguese meal at nearby **Café Nga Tim** (雅憩花園餐廳; 📞 853 2888 2086; 8 Rua do Caetano; mains MOP$80-250; ⏱ noon-1am). Enjoy the small-town atmosphere and, possibly, banter with the friendly owner – a guitar- and erhu-strumming ex-policeman named Feeling Wong. Before hopping back on the bus, grab a couple of egg-custard tarts from **Lord Stow's Bakery** (澳門安德魯餅店; 📞 853 2888 2534; 1 Rua da Tassara, Coloane; egg tarts MOP$9; ⏱ 7am-10pm).

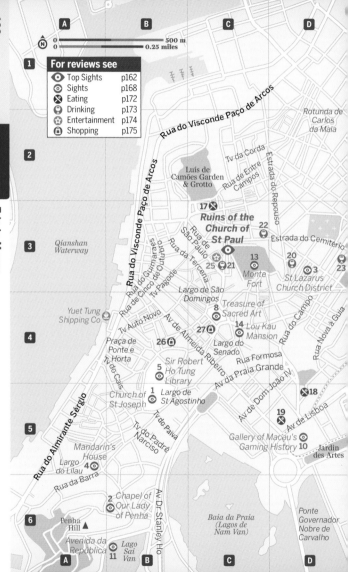

N

0 — 500 m
0 — 0.25 miles

For reviews see

- ◉ Top Sights p162
- ◎ Sights p168
- ✖ Eating p172
- 🍷 Drinking p173
- ★ Entertainment p174
- 🛍 Shopping p175

Rua do Visconde Paço de Arcos

Rua do Visconde Paço de Arcos

Rotunda de Carlos da Maia

Tv da Corda

Luís de Camões Garden & Grotto

Rua de Entre Campos

Estrada do Repouso

Qianshan Waterway

Rua do Visconde Paço de Arcos

17 ✖

Rua de São Paulo

Ruins of the Church of St Paul

22

Estrada do Cemitério

Rua da Tercena

Rua do Guimarães

Rua de Cinco de Outubro

Tv Pagode

25 ◎ **21**

13

Monte Fort

20

3 ◎

St Lazarus Church District

23

Yuet Tung Shipping Co

Largo de São Domingos

Tv Auto Novo

Av de Almeida Ribeiro

8 ◎

Treasure of Sacred Art

27 🛍

14 Lou Kau Mansion

Rua do Campo

Rua Nova à Guia

Praça de Ponte e Horta

26 🛍

Largo do Senado

Rua Formosa

Tv do Cais

Sir Robert Ho Tung Library

5 ◎

Av da Praia Grande

Av de Dom João IV

18 ✖

Church of St Joseph

1 ◎ Largo de St Agostinho

Tv do Paiva

19

Av de Lisboa

Rua do Almirante Sérgio

Tv do Padre Narciso

Gallery of Macau's Gaming History **10** ◎

Jardin des Artes

Mandarin's House

4 ◎

Largo do Lilau

Av Dr Stanley Ho

Baia da Praia (Lagos de Nam Van)

Ponte Governador Nobre de Carvalho

Rua da Barra

2 ◎ Chapel of Our Lady of Penha

Penha Hill ▲

Avenida da República

11 ◎ Lago Sai Van

Trip to Macau

🟢 24
Av do Coronel
Mesquita

Kun Iam 15
Temple

Estrada de Ferreira do amaral

Montanha
Russa
Garden

Rua dos Pescadores

Av do Ouvidor Arriaga

Av
Horta e Costa

Av do Conselheiro Ferreira de Almeida

Rua de Silva Mendes

Cemetery

16 ✖

Rua de Sidónio Pais

Cable Car
Terminus

Av de Sidónio Pais

Flora
Garden

Lou
Lim Ioc
Garden

Reservoir

🔺 Guia
Hill

9 Tap Seac
🎯 Gallery

Tap Seac
Square

Guia
Fortress
& Chapel
6 🎯

Guia Tunnel

Macau Maritime
Ferry Terminal

Outer Harbour
Ferry Terminal

Rua de Terminal
Marítimo

Heliport

Vasco
da Gama
Garden

Rua de Mallaca

12
🎯 AFA

Av do Dr Rodrigo Rodrigues

Rua de Nagasaki

Rua de Luís
Gonzaga Gomes

Av da Amizade · Avenida da Amizade

Fisherman's
Wharf

Rua de Pequim

Av da Amizade

Rua de Paris

Macau
Museum
7 of Art
🎯

Rua Cidade
de Santarém

NAPE

Rua de Roma

Macau
Cultural
Centre

Rua Cidade do Porto

Rua de Londres

Rua Cidade de Braga · Rua de Madrid

Av Dr Sun Yat Sen

Sights

Church of St Joseph   CHURCH

1 ◎ MAP P166, B5

St Joseph's, which falls outside the tourist circuit, is Macau's most beautiful model of tropicalised baroque architecture. Consecrated in 1758 as part of the Jesuit seminary, it features a scalloped canopy and a staircase leading to the courtyard from which you see the arresting white-and-yellow facade of the church and its dome. The latter is the oldest dome ever built in China. The interior, with its three altars, is lavishly ornamented with overlapping pilasters and attractive Solomonic 'spiral' columns. (聖若瑟聖堂, Capela do Seminario São José; Rua do Seminario; ◷10am-5pm; ☐9, 16, 18, 28B)

Chapel of Our Lady of Penha   HISTORIC BUILDING

2 ◎ MAP P166, B6

This graceful chapel atop Penha Hill was raised as a place of pilgrimage for Portuguese sailors in the 17th century, purportedly by survivors of a ship that had narrowly escaped capture by the Dutch. Most of what you see though came about in 1935. In the courtyard is a marble statue of Our Lady of Lourdes facing the sea; symmetrical staircases lead down to a grotto of the saint, complete with pews and altar. The grey chapel is visible across the lake. (西望洋聖母堂, Capela de Nossa Senhora da Penha; Top of Penha Hill; ◷9.30am-4pm; ☐3, 8, 9, 16)

St Lazarus Church District   AREA

3 ◎ MAP P166, D3

A lovely neighbourhood with colonial-style houses and cobbled streets makes for some of Macau's best photo ops. Designers and other creative types like to gather here, setting up shop and organising artsy events. (瘋堂斜巷, Calcada da Igreja de São Lázaro; www.cipa.org.mo; ☐7, 8)

Mandarin's House   HISTORIC BUILDING

4 ◎ MAP P166, A5

Built around 1869, the Mandarin's House, with over 60 rooms, was the ancestral home of Zheng Guanying, an influential author-merchant whose readers included emperors, Dr Sun Yatsen and Chairman Mao. The compound features a moon gate, tranquil courtyards, exquisite rooms and a main hall with French windows, all arranged in that labyrinthine-style typical of certain Chinese period buildings. There are guided tours in Cantonese on weekend afternoons. (鄭家大屋, Casa do Mandarim; ☎853 2896 8820; www.wh.mo/mandarinhouse; 10 Travessa de António da Silva; admission free; ◷10am-5.30pm Thu-Tue; ☐28B, 18)

Sir Robert Ho Tung Library

LIBRARY

5 MAP P166, B4

This charming building, founded in the 19th century, was the country retreat of the late tycoon Robert Ho Tung, who purchased it in 1918. The colonial edifice, featuring a dome, an arcaded facade, Ionic columns and Chinese-style gardens, was given a modern extension by architect Joy Choi Tin Tin in 2006. The new four-storey structure in glass and steel has Piranesi-inspired bridges connecting to the old house and a glass roof straddling the transitional space. (何東圖書館; 3 Largo de St Agostinho; ⏰8am-8pm Tue-Sun, from 2pm Mon; 🚌9, 16, 18)

Guia Fortress & Chapel

FORT, CHAPEL

6 MAP P166, E3

As the highest point on the peninsula, Guia Fortress affords panoramic views of the city. At the top is the small but stunning **Chapel of Our Lady of Guia**, built in 1622 and retaining almost 100% of its original features, including frescoes with both Portuguese and Chinese details that are among Asia's most important. Next to the chapel stands the oldest modern **lighthouse** (c 1865) on the China coast – an attractive 15m-tall structure that is usually closed to the public. (東望洋炮台及聖母雪地殿聖堂, Fortaleza da Guia e Capela de Guia; Flora Gardens; admission

Macau's Megacasinos

Cotai is Macau's answer to the Vegas Strip, an ever-growing collection of megacasinos and entertainment complexes drawing tens of millions of tourists every year. Even if you hate gambling, the casinos are marvels of giant-scale planning and detail – a faux Venice! A half-scale Eiffel Tower! Not to mention thrilling architecture – a beguiling art piece by Zaha Hadid! MGM Cotai, City of Dreams and Galaxy Macau are some of Cotai's most outrageous and ambitious casinos; the golden lotus-shaped tower of Grand Lisboa (p173) is a landmark on Macau Peninsula.

free; ⏰fortress 9am-6pm, chapel 10am-5.30pm, lighthouse open only on special days; 🚌2, 2A, 6A, 12, 17, 18, Flora Gardens stop)

Macau Museum of Art

MUSEUM

7 MAP P166, G5

This excellent five-storey museum has well-curated displays of art created in Macau and China, including paintings by western artists such as George Chinnery, who lived in the enclave. Other highlights are ceramics and stoneware excavated in Macau, Ming and Qing dynasty calligraphy from Guǎngdōng, ceramic statues from Shíwān (Guǎngdōng) and seal carvings. The museum also features 19th-century western historical paintings from all over

Asia, and contemporary Macanese art. (澳門藝術博物館, Museu de Arte de Macau; ☎853 8791 9814; www.mam.gov.mo; Macau Cultural Centre, Avenida Xian Xing Hai; admission free; ⏱10am-6.30pm Tue-Sun; 🚌1A, 8, 12, 23)

Treasure of Sacred Art   MUSEUM

8 ◉ MAP P166, C4

Northeast of Largo do Senado, the 17th-century baroque Church of St Dominic contains the Treasure of Sacred Art, an Aladdin's cave of ecclesiastical art and liturgical objects exhibited on three floors. The majority of the items were made in the 19th or early 20th-century in Macau or Portugal. You'll see doll-like statues of wood or ivory, precious rosary beads, and polychrome wood carvings of heads and limbs of saints stuffed in a

wooden chest. (聖物寶庫, Tresouro de Arte Sacra; Church of St Dominic, Largo de São Domingos; admission free; ⏱10am-6pm)

Tap Seac Gallery   GALLERY

9 ◉ MAP P166, E3

One of a handful of 1920s houses surrounding **Tap Seac Square** (塔石廣場, Praca do Tap Seac; 🚌7, 8), this one formerly belonging to an upper-class family has a European-style facade and Moorish arched doors. The gallery inside hosts excellent contemporary art exhibitions. The original patio in the middle of the house has been kept, which creates a light-filled, relaxing setting. (塔石藝文舘, Galeria Tap Seac; ☎853 2836 6866; www.icm.gov.mo/ts; 95 Avenida Conselheiro Ferreira

Cannon, Monte Fort

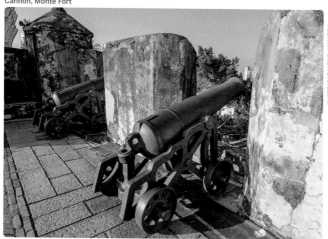

de Almeida; admission free; ⏰10am-9pm; 🚍7, 8)

Gallery of Macau's Gaming History

GALLERY

10 ◉ MAP P166, D5

Macau's gambling industry goes back to the 16th century, when labourers from China played a game called 'fan-tan' in makeshift stalls. While scholars have written about the subject, this is the first gallery devoted to it. The eye-opening exhibition walks you through Macau's gaming history via texts (Chinese only), fascinating old photos and vintage slot machines. (澳門博彩業歷史資料館; Crystal Palace Casino, 3rd fl, Hotel Lisboa, 2-4 Avenida de Lisboa; admission free; ⏰9am-5.30pm; 🚍3, 6, 26A)

Avenida da República

AREA

11 ◉ MAP P166, B6

Banyan-lined Avenida da República, along the northwest shore of Sai Van Lake, is Macau's oldest Portuguese quarter. There are several grand colonial villas not open to the public here. The former Bela Vista Hotel, one of the most-storied hotels in Asia, is now the **Residence of the Portuguese Consul-General** (葡國駐澳門領事官邸; Rua do Boa Vista). Nearby is the ornate **Santa Sancha Palace**, once the residence of Macau's Portuguese governors, and now used to accommodate dignitaries. Not too far away are beautiful, abandoned art deco–inspired buildings. (民國大馬路; 🚍6, 9, 16)

AFA

GALLERY

12 ◉ MAP P166, E4

Some of Macau's best contemporary art can be seen at this nonprofit gallery, which has taken Macau's art worldwide and holds monthly solo exhibitions by the city's top artists. AFA is near the Mong Há Multi-Sport Pavilion. Disembark from the bus at Rua da Barca or Rua de Francisco Xavier Pereira. Alternatively, it's a 20-minute walk from Largo do Senado. (全藝社, Art for All Society; 📞853 2836 6064; www.afamacau.com; 1st fl, Art Garden, 265 Avenida Dr Rodrigo Rodrigues; admission free; ⏰10am-7pm Mon-Fri; 🚍8, 8A, 18A, 7)

Monte Fort

FORT

13 ◉ MAP P166, C3

Just east of the Ruins of the Church of St Paul (p162), from which it is separated by a pebbled path and picturesque foliage, Monte Fort was built by the Jesuits between 1617 and 1626 to defend the College of the Mother of God against pirates. It was later handed over to the colonial government. Barracks and storehouses were designed to allow the fort to survive a two-year siege, but the cannons were fired only once, during the aborted attempt by the Dutch to invade Macau in 1622. (大炮台, Fortaleza do Monte; Praceta do Museu de Macau; admission free; ⏰7am-7pm; 🚍7, 8, disembark at Social Welfare Bureau)

Lou Kau Mansion HISTORIC BUILDING

14 🎯 MAP P166, C4

Built around 1889, this Cantonese-style mansion with southern European elements belonged to merchant Lou Wa Sio (aka Lou Kau), who also commissioned the **Lou Lim leoc Garden** (盧廉若公園; http://en.macaotourism.gov.mo). Behind the grey facade, an intriguing maze of open and semi-enclosed spaces blurs the line between inside and outside. The flower-and-bird motif on the roof can also be found in the Mandarin's House and A-Ma Temple. Traditional craft workers often practise their art here during weekdays. (盧家大屋, Casa de Lou Kau; 📞 853 8399 6699; www.wh.mo/loukau; 7 Travessa da Sé; admission free; ⏰ 10am-5.30pm Tue-Sun; 🚌 3, 4, 6A, 8A, 19, 33)

Kun Iam Temple BUDDHIST TEMPLE

15 🎯 MAP P166, E1

Macau's oldest temple was founded in the 13th century, but the present structures date to 1627. The roof ridges are ornately embellished with porcelain figurines and the halls are lavishly decorated, if a little weathered. Inside the main hall stands the likeness of Kun Iam, the Goddess of Mercy; to the left of the altar is a bearded arhat rumoured to represent Marco Polo. The first Sino-American treaty was signed at a round stone table in the temple's terraced gardens in 1844. (觀音廟, Templo de Kun Iam; 2 Avenida do Coronel Mesquita; ⏰ 7am-5.30pm; 🚌 1A, 10, 18A, stop Travessa de Venceslau de Morais)

Eating

Riquexó Cafe CAFETERIA $

16 🍴 MAP P166, F2

Modest Riquexó is *the* place for tasty, no-frills Macanese. Take your pick of the daily options, which may include *minchi,* a homey dish of minced meat sautéed with diced potatoes, and seasoned with soy and Worcester sauce. Then sit down in the cafe and look at the old photos of Macau on the white tiled walls as you wait for your order. (利多咖啡屋; 📞 853 2856 5655; 69 Avenida Sidonio Pais; meals from MOP$60; ⏰ noon-10pm)

Hou Kong Chi Kei CANTONESE $

17 🍴 MAP P166, C3

Local families have been flocking to this unassuming restaurant for reasonably priced barbecued fish and pig-ear salad even before it received a Michelin mention. Now reservation is a must on weekends. The fried taro fish balls and chunky oyster omelette are served piping hot and go swimmingly with Tsingtao beer. (濠江志記; 📞 853 2895 3098; Ground fl, Block 3, Lai Hou Gardens, Rua Coelho do Amaral; dishes MOP$48-228; ⏰ 6.30-10.30pm; 🚌 8A, 17, 26)

Clube Militar de Macau PORTUGUESE $$

18 🍴 MAP P166, D5

In a distinguished colonial building, with fans spinning lazily above,

Eight restaurant, Grand Lisboa casino

the Military Club takes you back in time to a quieter Macau. Simple and delicious Portuguese fare is complemented by reasonably priced wines and cheeses. The MOP$200 lunch buffet is great value, though à la carte offers more culinary refinement and a chance to taste the famous *leitão* (suckling pig). (陸軍俱樂部; ☎853 2871 4000; 975 Avenida da Praia Grande; meals MOP$200-500; ☺1.45-2.45pm & 7-10.30pm Mon-Fri, noon-2pm & 7-10.30pm Sat & Sun; ❄; ☒6, 28C)

Eight   CANTONESE $$$

19 ⊗ MAP P166, D5

The Eight is a stellar three-Michelin star restaurant and model of Cantonese culinary refinement inside the Grand Lisboa. You can dine on a 'simple' meal of roast meat and Cantonese soup cooked to perfection, or splurge on marine delicacies such as abalone, to the accompaniment of water cascading down a wall and crystal-dripping chandeliers. Reservation a must. (8餐廳; ☎853 8803 7788; www.grandlisboahotel.com; 2nd fl, Grand Lisboa Hotel, Avenida de Lisboa; main dishes MOP$480-3000; ☺lunch 11.30am-2.30pm Mon-Sat, brunch 10am-3pm Sun, dinner 6.30-10.30pm daily; ℗❄🛜; ☒3, 10, 28B)

Drinking

Beer Temple   PUB

20 🍺 MAP P166, D3

As the name suggests, the craft beer selection here is huge. If you can't decide, tell the staff your preference – fruit-forward, dry and bitter, or smelling like a pine forest – and they'll pick something out for you. Consume in the bar area with the high ceiling, loud music and shiny black surfaces. (☎853 2835 2803; www.facebook.com/beertemple.patiolazaro/; 4 Pátio São Lázaro; ⏱noon-2am; 🛜; 🚍3, 4, 6A, 19)

Macau Soul   BAR

21 🅿 MAP P166, C3

An elegant haven in wood and stained glass, where twice a month a jazz band plays to a packed audience. On most nights, though, Thelonious Monk fills the air as customers chat with the owners and dither over their 400 Portuguese wines that include some rare varietals. Opening hours vary; phone ahead. Cash only. (澳感廊; ☎853 2836 5182; www.macausoul.com; 31A Rua de São Paulo; ⏱3-10pm Wed & Thu, to midnight Fri-Sun; 🚍8A, 17, 26)

Che Che Cafe   BAR

22 🅿 MAP P166, C3

Owned by a member of post-rock band Why Oceans, Che Che is reassuringly dimly lit and laid-back. A faux-antique world map and a neon sign lamenting 'Love Will Tear Us Apart' jump out from dark walls. You may see culturally minded youth discussing film over a bottle of sake or pints of frothy beer. (☎853 6288 0857; www.face-book.com/chechecafemacau; 70A Rua de Tomás Vieira; ⏱3pm-2am Mon-Sat; 🚍7, 8, 18A, 19)

Single Origin   COFFEE

23 🅿 MAP P166, D3

This airy corner cafe opened by coffee professional Keith Fong makes a mean shot of espresso. You can choose your poison (single origin, of course) from a daily selection of 10 beans. If you can't decide, the well-trained baristas are more than happy to help. (單品; ☎853 6698 7475; 19 Rua de Abreu Nunes; coffee MOP$35; ⏱noon-8pm; 🛜; 🚍2, 4, 7, 7A, 8)

Entertainment

Live Music Association   LIVE MUSIC

24 ⭐ MAP P166, E1

The go-to place for indie music in Macau, this excellent dive inside an industrial building hosts live acts from Macau and overseas. There are two or three bands a week, with past performers including Cold Cave, Buddhiston, Mio Myo and Pet Conspiracy. See its Facebook page for what's on. (LMA; 現場音樂協會; ☎853 2875 7511; www.facebook.com/lma.macau; 11th fl, Flat B, San Mei Industrial Bldg, 50 Avenida do Coronel Mesquita; 🚍7, 17, 18B)

Cinematheque Passion   CINEMA

25 ⭐ MAP P166, C3

An attractive yellow house shelters Macau's art-house cinema and film archive. There are regular screenings of Macanese movies and films about the city. But even if you're not here for the flicks, it's

House of Dancing Water

Macau's most expensively made show is **The House of Dancing Water** (水舞間; ☎853 8868 6688; http://thehouseofdancingwater.com; City of Dreams, Estrada do Istmo, Cotai; tickets MOP$580-1480; 🚌50, 35)' – a breathtaking melange of stunts, acrobatics and theatre designed by Franco Dragone, the former director of Cirque du Soleil. The magic revolves around a cobalt pool the size of several Olympic-sized swimming pools. Over, around, into and under this pool a cast of 80, dressed in glorious costumes, perform hair-raising stunts.

worth going through the lobby to the back to see the garden with the shapely trees and a view of the Ruins of the Church of St Paul. Most films come with English subtitles. (戀愛電影館; ☎853 2852 2585; www.cinematheque-passion. mo; 11-13 Travessa da Paixão; tickets adult/student & senior MOP$60/30; ⏱ticket office 10am-11.30pm, archive 10am-8pm Tue-Sun; 🚌2, 3, 4, 6, 7)

Shopping

LCM Shop of Canned Macau
FOOD

26 🔒 MAP P166, B4

This beautiful shop carries dozens of canned seafood brands (representing hundreds of varieties) from Portugal, all labelled with details on the history of the maker and the product. You'll find not only excellent sardine, tuna and mackerel, but also sea bream, *bacalhau* (salted cod), octopus

and *sangacho de atum* (tuna blood). The last is good on a bed of greens with citrus dressing. (澳門葡式辣魚店, LCM Loja das Conservas Macau; ☎853 6571 8214; www.face-book.com/lojasconservasmacau; 9 Travessa do Aterro Novo; MOP$30-300; ⏱11am-9pm; 🚌4, 8A, 18A, 19)

Pin-to Livros e Musica
BOOKS

27 🔒 MAP P166, C4

One of Macau's best independent bookshops, Pin-to (which means 'where' in Cantonese) has a strong curation of titles in art and culture, including some in Portuguese and in English. The collections reflect the taste of owner Anson who can sometimes be seen reading by the staircase. You'll also find a dozen or so jazz and esoteric CDs, and two resident cats. (邊度有書有音樂; ☎853 2833 0909; www.facebook.com/pg/pintolivros; 47 Estrada de Coelho do Amaral; ⏱noon-9pm Tue-Sun; 🚌3, 6, 26A)

Survival Guide

Central District (p35) TUNGCHEUNG / SHUTTERSTOCK ©

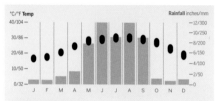

When to Go

Spring (Mar–May) Lots of festivals, including Asia's top film festival, the Rugby Sevens tournament, Art Basel and deities' birthdays.

Summer (Jun–Aug) Swelteringly hot and rainy; the best time to see dragon boat races in between trips to the beach.

Autumn (Sep–Nov) October to December is the best time to visit Hong Kong, but beware of typhoons in September.

Winter (Dec–Feb) Chilly with occasional rain, Hong Kong celebrates Chinese New Year under Christmas lights.

Before You Go

Book Your Stay

○ Hong Kong accommodation is expensive but there's plenty of diversity, from dorm beds to chic apartments and palatial suites.

○ Most hotels on Hong Kong Island are between Sheung Wan and Causeway Bay; in Kowloon, they fall around Nathan Rd, where you'll also find budget places.

○ All rooms have air-conditioning, and all but the cheapest rooms have private bathrooms, free in-room wi-fi and cable TV in English.

Useful Websites

Lonely Planet (lonelyplanet.com/china/hong-kong/hotels) Hostels, B&B and hotel listings, and an online booking service.

Hong Kong Hotels Association (香港酒店業協會; HKHA; ☑ 852 2769 8822, 852 2383 8380; www.hkha.org; Hong Kong International Airport; ☉ 7am-midnight) For booking midrange and high-end hotels that are members of the association.

Discover Hong Kong (www.discoverhongkong.com) The tourist board's website has a large database of hotels, including those accredited by the Quality Tourism Services scheme, searchable by location and facilities.

Best Budget

Hop Inn on Carnavon (www.hopinn.hk) Local art murals, sofas and a beer fridge sum up this Kowloon hostel.

Mojo Nomad (www.mojonomad.com) Magnificent water views complemented by offbeat design.

Helena May (www.helenamay.com) Simple heritage rooms (some female-only) in a Central institution.

SLEEEP (www.sleeep.io) Eco-conscious capsule hotel with just eight beds and fancy gadgets in an expensive area.

Mini Hotel Central (www.minihotel.hk/

central) Tiny rooms but plush lounge and hard-to-beat location slap bang in the middle of Central.

Best Midrange

Twenty One Whitfield (www.twentyonewhitfield.com) Clean, bright rooms available for daily and monthly stays in Tin Hau.

Tuve (www.tuve.hk) Sleek, industrial-chic rooms, an artsy reception area, and helpful staff in Tin Hau.

99 Bonham (www.99bonham.com) Impeccable taste in a great location.

Hotel Jen (www.hoteljen.com/hongkong) The best deal on Hong Kong Island with a rooftop pool, in a pleasingly local area.

Little Tai Hang (www.littletaihang.com) Charming hotel with Scandi-style furnishings in an equally charming neighbourhood.

Best Top End

Peninsula Hong Kong (www.peninsula.com) One of the most elegant and richly storied hotels in Asia.

Hotel Indigo (www.ihg.com) Chinese-inspired design, state-of-the-art facilities and exceptional service make this a winner.

Hotel Icon (www.hotel-icon.com) Affordable luxury with a rooftop pool.

Murray Hotel (www.niccolohotels.com) A pioneering luxury reinvention of a heritage building in Central.

Fleming (www.theflem ing.com) An updated classic, with design flourishes that mimic Hong Kong's beloved retro ferries.

Arriving in Hong Kong

Hong Kong International Airport

Hong Kong International Airport (HKG; ☏ 852 2181 8888; www.hkairport.com) Airport Express MTR train to city centre from 5.54am to 12.48am, HK$110 (with Octopus) or HK$115; 'A' buses to various parts of Hong Kong from 6am to 12.30am, HK$19 to HK$45; taxi to Central/Kowloon around HK$370/270.

Lo Wu and Lok Ma Chau MTR train to city

Tickets & Passes

Octopus (www.octopuscards.com) This prepaid travel card can be used on most forms of public transport, saves you 5% on fares, and is a convenient way to pay. You can buy one and recharge at any MTR station.

Airport Express Travel Pass (one way/return HK$250/350) As well as travel to/from the airport, it allows three consecutive days of mostly unlimited travel on the MTR, Light Rail and MTR Bus.

MTR Tourist Day Pass (adult/child three to 11 years HK$65/30) Valid on the MTR for 24 hours after the first use.

centre from 5.55am to midnight (Lo Wu), from 6.38am to 10.55pm (Lok Ma Chau), HK$44 to HK$53.

Hong Kong–Macau Ferry Terminal

○ MTR train (Sheung Wan) to Central/Kowloon from 6.05am to 12.56am, HK$5 to HK$10; taxi HK$24 to HK$100.

China Ferry Terminal

○ Star Ferry to Central from 6.30am to

11.30pm, HK$2.20 to HK$3.70; taxi HK$34 to HK$44.

West Kowloon Train Terminus

○ The West Kowloon high-speed rail terminus opened in September 2018, comprising joint immigration and customs for travel to mainland China.

○ High-speed direct trains depart from here to Shēnzhèn, Guǎngzhōu South, Běijīng West and Shànghǎi Hóngqiáo stations.

Getting Around

Metro

The Mass Transit Railway is the name for Hong Kong's rail system comprising underground, overland and Light Rail (slower tram-style) services. Universally known as the 'MTR', it is clean, fast and safe.

○ Fares cost HK$4 to HK$25 and it is the quickest way to get to

Taxi

Hong Kong taxis are a bargain compared with those in other world-class cities, and always use their meter.

Language Some taxi drivers speak English well, but many don't. It's never a bad idea to have your destination written down in Chinese.

Availability Taxis are easy to flag down except during rush hour, when it rains, or during the driver shift-change period (around 4pm daily). When available, there should be a red 'For Hire' sign illuminated in the front windscreen.

Fares Urban taxis (red) charge HK$24 for the first 2km and HK$1.70 for every 200m and minute of wait time thereafter (reducing to HK$1.20 if the fare exceeds HK$83.50).

Paying Try to carry smaller bills and coins; most drivers are hesitant to make change for HK$500. You can tip up to 10%, but it's not generally expected.

From the airport Expect to pay around HK$270 to Kowloon and around HK$350 to central Hong Kong Island, plus HK$6 for each piece of luggage carried in the baggage compartment.

most destinations in Hong Kong.

○ Routes, timetables and fares can be found at www.mtr.com.hk.

Bus

Hong Kong's extensive bus system will take you just about any-where in the territory, but it's not always easy to follow. Most useful for the southern side of Hong Kong Island, the New Territories and Lantau Island.

Departures Most buses run from 5.30am or 6am until midnight or 12.30am. There are a small number of night buses that run from 12.45am to 5am or later, designated with the letter 'N'.

Fares Bus fares cost HK$4 to HK$46, depending on the destination. Fares for night buses cost from HK$7 to HK$32. You will need exact change or an Octopus card.

Route information Figuring out which bus you want can be difficult. Citybus (www. nwstbus.com.hk) and New World First Bus, owned by the same company, plus Kowloon

Motor Bus (www.kmb. hk) provide user-friendly route searches on their websites. KMB also has a route app for smartphones.

Ferry

The cross-harbour Star Ferry (p36) services are faster and cheaper than buses and the MTR.

○ There are two Star Ferry routes, but by far the most popular is the one running between Central (Pier 7) and Tsim Sha Tsui. The other links Wan Chai with Tsim Sha Tsui.

○ There are two ticket types; upper deck (slightly more expensive) and lower deck. Fares are nominally higher on weekends and public holidays.

○ Buy a ticket at one of the payment kiosks or use an Octopus card (most convenient).

Tram

Hong Kong's vener-able old trams are tall, narrow double-deckers. They are slow, but they're cheap and a great way to explore the city above ground level.

○ The flat fare is HK$2.60 for adults,

HK$1.30 for kids. Drop your coins (exact change only) into the box beside the driver, or use the Octopus touch pad.

○ Use the turnstiles at the back of the trams to get on; pay at the front when you disembark.

○ The route is very simple, moving along one set of tracks that runs along the northern coast of Hong Kong Island (with a couple of minor offshoots), from Kennedy Town in the west to Shau Kei Wan in the east.

Essential Information

Accessible Travel

People with mobility issues face substantial obstacles in Hong Kong, particularly on Hong Kong Island, be-cause of its extremely hilly topography, pedestrian overpasses and crowded – often obstructed – streets. Those with hearing or visual impairments will find several aids to help them, including Braille panels in lift lobbies and audio units at traffic signals.

Business Hours

Banks 9am to 4.30pm or 5.30pm Monday to Friday, 9am to 12.30pm Saturday.

Museums 10am to between 5pm and 9pm; many close on Mondays as well as sometimes Sundays.

Offices 9am to 5.30pm or 6pm Monday to Friday (lunch hour 1pm to 2pm).

Restaurants 11am to 3pm and 6pm to 11pm.

Shops Usually 10am to 8pm.

Electricity

Type G
220V/50Hz

Emergencies

o Fire, police and ambulance (☎999)

o Weather/tropical cyclone warning enquiries (☎187 8200)

Money

ATMs

o Most ATMs are linked up to international money systems such as Cirrus, Maestro, Plus and Visa Electron.

o Withdrawal fees will typically be between HK$20 and HK$50 per transaction, and the local ATM provider may levy an extra surcharge.

o American Express (Amex) cardholders can withdraw cash from AEON ATMs in Hong Kong if they have signed up to Amex Express Cash service before arrival.

Credit Cards

o Credit (and debit) cards are widely used in midrange to upmarket shops, restaurants and bars, and it is safe to pay with them.

o The most widely accepted cards are Visa, MasterCard, Amex, Diners Club and JCB – pretty much in that

order. It may be an idea to carry two, just in case.

Local Currency

Hong Kong uses the Hong Kong dollar (HK$); Macau uses pataca but most places accept Hong Kong currency as well.

Tipping

Hotels A HK$10 or HK$20 note for the porter at luxury hotels; gratuity for cleaning staff at your discretion.

Restaurants Most eateries, except very cheap places, impose a 10% to 15% service charge. At budget joints, just rounding off to the nearest HK$10 is fine.

Bars and cafes Not expected unless table service is provided, in which case 10% will often be automatically added to your bill.

Safe Travel

Hong Kong is generally a safe city to travel around, even alone at night, but always use common sense.

After dark Stick to well-lit streets if walking; note the MTR is perfectly safe to use at night.

Theft Hong Kong has its share of pickpockets. Carry as little cash and as few valuables as possible, and if you put a bag down, keep an eye on it. If robbed, obtain a loss report for insurance purposes at the nearest police station. See 'e-Report Room' at www.police.gov.hk.

Telephone Services

More and more hotels are including free mobile handsets with 4G data and free local calls as part of the room deal.

○ Any GSM-compatible phone can be used here. If you have an unlocked handset, buying a local SIM card with 4G mobile data and free local calls is convenient and easy.

○ The Hong Kong Tourist Board sells a prepaid Tourist SIM, which includes 4G mobile data, unlimited CSL wi-fi hotspot usage and unlimited calls; CSL stores and 7-Elevens have other options.

○ Buy an International Direct Dial (IDD) Global Calling Card for cheaper rates on global calls; they are available at CSL and 7-Eleven stores.

Toilets

○ Hong Kong has a vast number of free western-style public toilets.

○ Hong Kong's Toilet Rush mobile app will show you where the nearest public toilets are to your location.

Tourist Information

Hong Kong International Airport (Chek Lap Kok; ⏰7am-11pm) In Halls A and B on the arrivals level in Terminal 1, and the E2 transfer area.

The Peak (港島旅客諮詢及服務中心; www.dis coverhongkong.com; Peak Piazza, The Peak; ⏰11am-8pm; Peak Tram) In a vintage tram, between the Peak Tower and the Peak Galleria.

Kowloon (香港旅遊發展局; Star Ferry Concourse, Tsim Sha Tsui; ⏰8am-8pm; Star Ferry) On the Star Ferry Visitor Concourse, right by the ferry terminal.

Lo Wu (羅湖旅客諮詢及服務中心; 2nd fl, Arrival Hall, Lo Wu Terminal Bldg, New Territories; ⏰8am-6pm) At this border crossing to Shēnzhèn, mainland China.

Visas

Visas are not required for Brits (up to 180 days), or Australians, Canadians, EU citizens, Israelis, Japanese, New Zealanders and US citizens (up to 90 days).

Wi-fi Hotspots

Free wi-fi is available in virtually all hotels, cafes and bars, at the airport, in MTR stations, on some buses and in various public areas. There are more than 15,000 public hotspots in Hong Kong. They will pop up as 'CSL' or 'Wi.Fi.HK' on your device; you can search where the latter hotspots are by downloading the Wi.Fi.HK mobile app.

Language

Cantonese is the most popular Chinese dialect in Hong Kong. Cantonese speakers can read Chinese characters, but will pronounce many characters differently from a Mandarin speaker.

Cantonese has 'tonal' quality – the raising and lowering of pitch on certain syllables. Tones fall on vowels and on the consonant **n**. Our pronunciation guides show five tones, indicated by accent marks – **à** (high), **á** (high rising), **à** (low falling), **á** (low rising), **a** (low) – plus a level tone (**a**).

To enhance your trip with a phrasebook, visit **lonelyplanet.com**.

Basics

Hello.	哈佬。	hàa·ló
Goodbye.	再見。	joy·gin
How are you?	你好嘛？	náy hó maa
Fine.	幾好。	gáy hó
Please ...	唔該……	ǹg·gòy ...
Thank you.	多謝。	dàw·je
Excuse me.	對唔住。	deui·ǹg·jew
Sorry.	對唔住。	deui·ǹg·jew
Yes.	係。	hai
No.	不係。	ǹg·hai

Do you speak English?

你識唔識講　　láy sìk·ǹg·sìk
英文啊？　　　gáwng
　　　　　　　yìng·mán aa

I don't understand.

我唔明。　　　ngáw ǹg mìng

Eating & Drinking

I'd like..., please.

唔該我要……　　ǹg·gòy ngáw yiu ...

a table for two	兩位嘅檯	léung wái ge tóy
the drink list	酒料單	jáu·líu·dàan
the menu	菜單	choy·dàan
beer	啤酒	bè·jáu
coffee	咖啡	gaa·fè

I don't eat ...

我唔吃……　　ngáw ǹg sik ...

fish	魚	yéw
poultry	雞鴨鵝	gài ngaap ngàw
red meat	牛羊肉	ngàu yèung yuk

Cheers!

乾杯！　　　gàwn·bui

That was delicious.

真好味。　　　jàn hó·may

I'd like the bill, please.

唔該我要　　ǹg·gòy ngáw yiu
埋單。　　　màai·dàan

Shopping

I'd like to buy ...

我想買……　　ngáw séung máai

I'm just looking.

睇下。　　　tái hạa

How much is it?
幾多錢？　　　　　*gáy·dàw chín*

That's too expensive.
太貴啦。　　　　　*taai gwai laa*

Can you lower the price?
可唔可以平 啲呀？ *háw·ǹg·háw·yí pèng
dì aa*

Emergencies

Help!　　　　救命！　*gau·mẹng*

Go away!　　　走開！　*jáu·hòy*

Call a doctor!　快啲叫醫生!
faai·dì giu yì·sàng

Call the police! 快啲叫警察!
faai·dì giu gíng·chaat

I'm lost.　　　我蕩失路。
ngáw dạwng·sàk·lọ

I'm sick.　　　我病咗。
ngáw bẹng·jáw

Where are the toilets?
廁所喺邊度？ *chi·sáw hái bìn·dọ*

Time & Numbers

What time is it?
而家 幾點鐘？ *yi·gàa gáy·dím·jùng*

It's (10) o'clock.
(十)點鐘。　*(sạp)·dím·jùng*

Half past (10).
(十)點半。　*(sạp)·dím bun*

morning　　朝早　　*jiù·jó*

afternoon　下晝　　*hạa·jau*

evening　　夜晚　　*ye·mǎan*

yesterday　寢日　　*kàm·yạt*

today　　　今日　　*gàm·yạt*

tomorrow　听日　　*tìng·yạt*

1	一	*yàt*
2	二	*yị*
3	三	*sàam*
4	四	*say*
5	五	*ńg*
6	六	*lụk*
7	七	*chàt*
8	八	*baat*
9	九	*gáu*
10	十	*sạp*

Transport & Directions

Where's ...?
……喺邊度？ *... hái bìn·dọ*

What's the address?
地址係？ *day·jí hại*

How do I get there?
點樣去？ *dím·yéung heui*

How far is it?
有幾遠？ *yáu gáy yéwn*

Can you show me (on the map)?
你可唔可以 *láy háw·ǹg·háw·yí*
(喺地圖度)指俾 *(hái dạy·tọ dọ) jí báy*
我睇我喺邊度？ *ngáw tái ngáw hái bìn·dọ*

When's the next bus?
下一班巴士 幾點開？
hạa·yàt·bàan bàa·sí gáy dím hòy

A ticket to ...
一張去…… 嘅飛。 *yàt jèung heui ...ge fày*

Does it stop at ...?
會唔會喺……停呀? *wuị·ǹg·wuị hái ...
tìng aa*

I'd like to get off at ...
我要喺…… 落車。*ngáw yiu hái ...
lạwk·chè*

Behind the Scenes

Send Us Your Feedback

We love to hear from travellers – your comments help make our books better. We read every word, and we guarantee that your feedback goes straight to the authors. Visit **lonelyplanet.com/contact** to submit your updates and suggestions.

Note: We may edit, reproduce and incorporate your comments in Lonely Planet products such as guidebooks, websites and digital products, so let us know if you don't want your comments reproduced or your name acknowledged. For a copy of our privacy policy visit lonelyplanet.com/privacy.

Lorna's Thanks

As always, huge thanks to the family that kept things together while I disappeared into the sub-tropics to do this update, especially my husband Rob who never baulks when I tell him how long my research trips are going to be. Thanks also to the enthusiastic Hong Kongers I met during my trip, who were full of recommendations and tips over dim sum and jazz. Last but not least, thanks to Austin and Lily for waiting patiently for my return home.

Acknowledgements

Cover photograph: Junk sailing on Victoria Harbour, Maurizio Rellini/4Corners ©

This Book

This 7th edition of Lonely Planet's *Pocket Hong Kong* guidebook was researched and written by Lorna Parkes, Piera Chen and Thomas O'Malley. The previous edition was written by Piera Chen and Emily Matchar. This guidebook was produced by the following:

Destination Editor
Megan Eaves

Senior Product Editor
Kate Chapman

Product Editor
Shona Gray

Senior Cartographer
Julie Sheridan

Book Designer
Wibowo Rusli

Assisting Editors Min Dai, Carly Hall, Trent Holden, Kellie Langdon, Anne Mulvaney, Monique Perrin

Cover Researcher
Wibowo Rusli

Thanks to Grace Dobell, Alison Lyall, Amanda Williamson, Juan Winata

Index

See also separate subindexes for:

- 🍴 **Eating p190**
- 🍷 **Drinking p190**
- 🎭 **Entertainment p191**
- 🛍️ **Shopping p191**

Index

Our Writers

Lorna Parkes

Londoner by birth and Melburnian by palate, Lorna has contributed to numerous Lonely Planet books and magazines. She's discovered she writes best on planes, and is most content when researching food and booze. Wineries and the tropics (not at the same time!) are her go-to happy places, but Yorkshire will always be special to her. Follow her @Lorna_Explorer.

Piera Chen

Piera is a travel writer who divides her time among Hong Kong (hometown), Taiwan and Vancouver when not on the road. She has authored over a dozen travel guides and contributed to as many travel-related titles. Piera is also a film reviewer, translator and poet, whose works have appeared in *The Hollywood Reporter*, *Cha Asian Literary Journal*, and other publications. Follow her @PieraChen.

Thomas O'Malley

A British writer based in Beijing, Tom is a world-leading connoisseur of cheap eats, dive bars, dark alleyways and hangovers. He has contributed travel stories to everyone from the BBC to *Playboy*, and reviews hotels for the *Telegraph*. Under another guise, he is a comedy scriptwriter. Follow him by walking behind at a distance. Tom tweets @Beijing_gourmet.

Published by Lonely Planet Global Limited
CRN 554153
7th edition – June 2019
ISBN 978 1 78657 809 9
© Lonely Planet 2019   Photographs © as indicated 2019
10 9 8 7 6 5 4 3 2 1
Printed in Malaysia